SRA PHONICS 2

Alvin Granowsky, Ed.D.

CONTRIBUTING AUTHORS

Joy Ann Tweedt, classroom teacher
Norman Najimy, educational consultant

REVIEWERS

Dr. Helen Brown
Director of Elementary Programs, K-8
Metropolitan Public Schools
Nashville, Tennessee

Nora Forester
Reading Coordinator, K-8
Northside Independent School District
San Antonio, Texas

Pamela K. Francis
Principal
Seltice Elementary School
Post Falls, Idaho

SRA

Macmillan/McGraw-Hill

Contents

Project Supervisor: Deborah Akers
Production Design and Development: PAT CUSICK and ASSOCIATES
Design Director: LESIAK/CRAMPTON DESIGN INC.

ISBN 002-686010-4

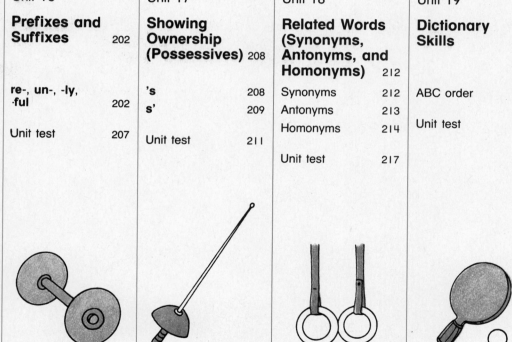

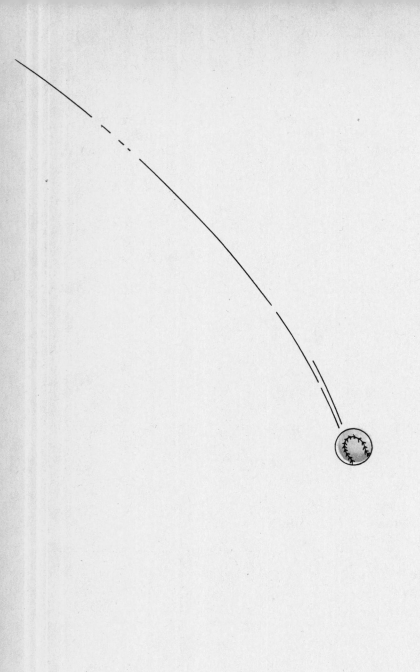

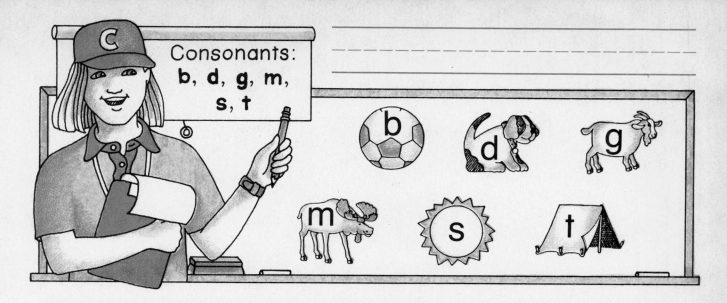

Consonants:
b, d, g, m, s, t

1 🗣 Say each picture name.
2 👂 Listen to the first sound.
3 ✏️ Print the letter that stands for the first sound.

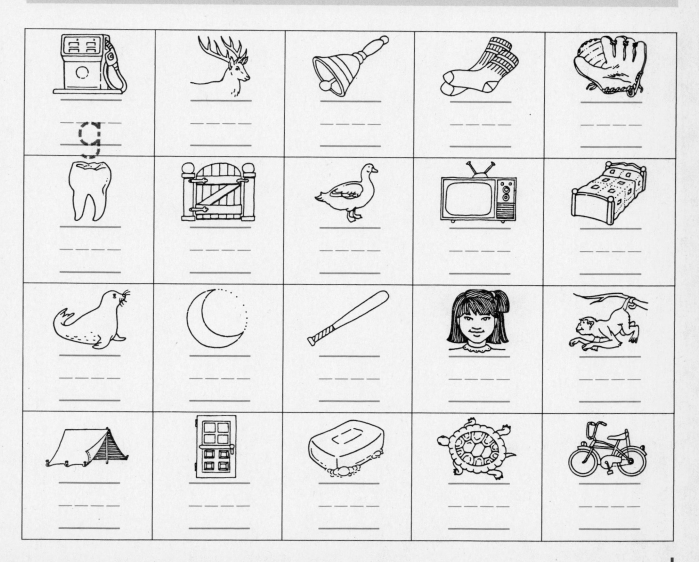

Consonants:
b, d, g, m, s, t

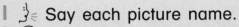

1. 🗣 Say each picture name.
2. 👂 Listen to the last sound.
3. ✏ Print the letter that stands for the last sound.

Using the consonant sounds of **b, d, g, m, s, t** in final position

1 🗣 Say each picture name.
2 👂 Listen to the middle sound.
3 ✏ Print the letter that stands for the middle sound.

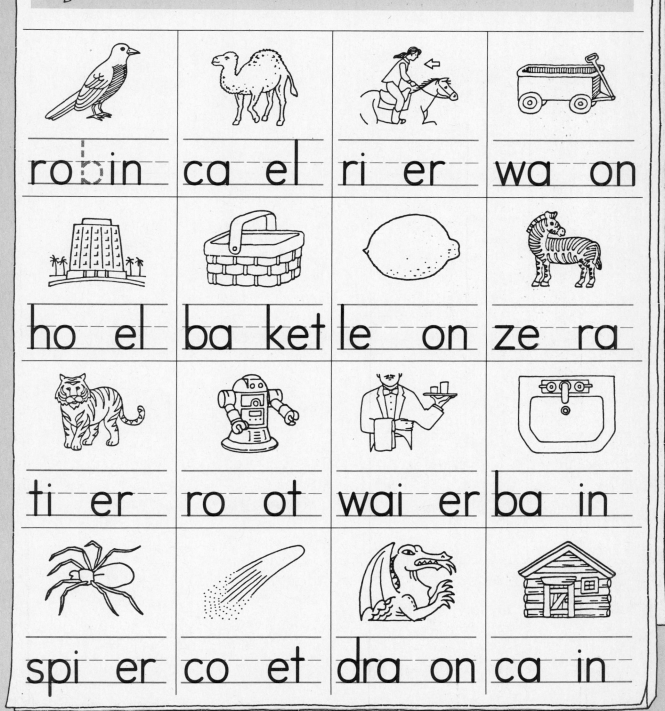

ro b in	ca el	ri er	wa on
ho el	ba ket	le on	ze ra
ti er	ro ot	wai er	ba in
spi er	co et	dra on	ca in

1 Say the sound each letter stands for.
2 Listen to that sound in each picture name.
3 Print the letter to show where you hear that sound in the picture name.

s	m	g	d
t	b	d	m
g	t	s	b
d	s	m	t
b	d	t	m

4

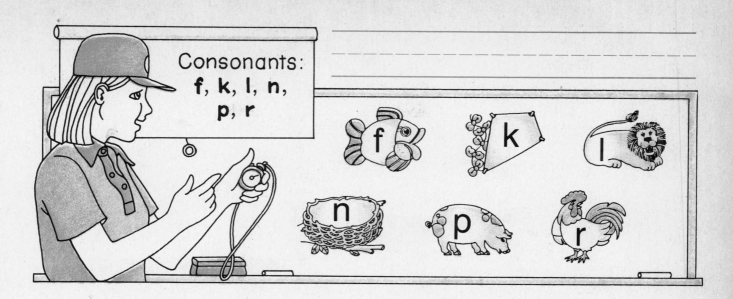

Consonants:
f, k, l, n, p, r

1. 🗣 Say each picture name.
2. 👂 Listen to the first sound.
3. ✏ Print the letter that stands for the first sound.

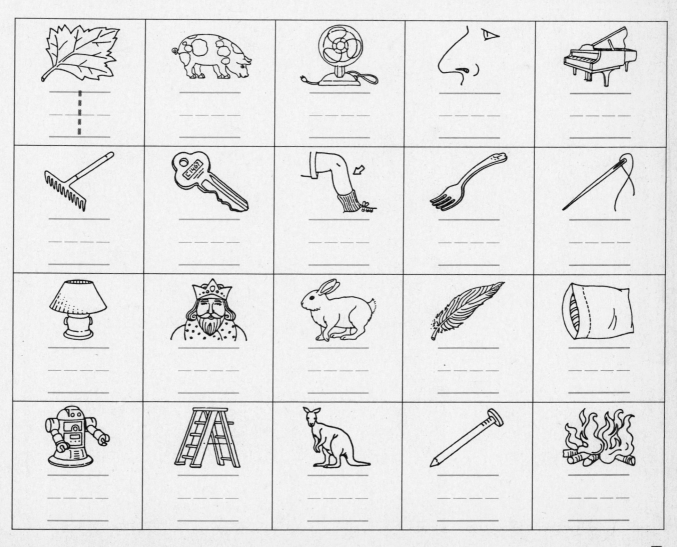

Consonants:
f, k, l, n, p, r

1 Say each picture name.
2 Listen to the last sound.
3 Print the letter that stands for the last sound.

Using the consonant sounds of **f, k, l, n, p, r** in final position

1 🗣 Say each picture name.
2 👂 Listen to the middle sound.
3 ✏ Print the letter that stands for the middle sound.

ru __ er	fe __ der	so __ a	pa __ er
wi __ ter	ze __ o	tu __ ip	ga __ den
o __ en	fi __ teen	pa __ ty	mo __ ey
ba __ er	me __ on	blan __ et	na __ kin

1 Say the sound each letter stands for.
2 Listen to that sound in each picture name.
3 Print the letter to show where you hear that sound in the picture name.

8

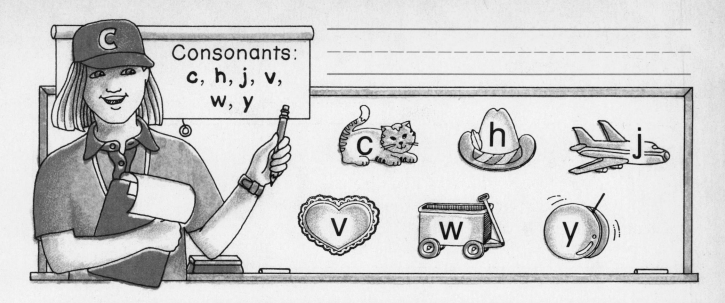

Consonants:
c, h, j, v,
w, y

1 Say each picture name.
2 Listen to the first sound.
3 Print the letter that stands for the first sound.

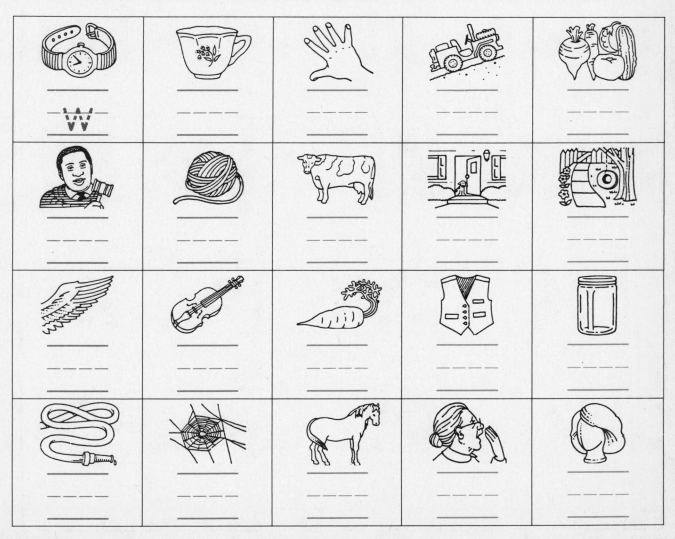

Introducing the consonant sounds of **c**, **h**, **j**, **v**, **w**, **y**

Consonants:
c, h, j, v, w, y

1. 🗣 Say the sound each letter stands for.
2. 👂 Listen to that sound in each picture name.
3. ✏️ Print the letter to show where you hear that sound in the picture name.

v	y	c	w
w	h	j	v
v	c	v	h
j	c	w	c
v	y	c	v

10

Reviewing the consonant sounds of **c, h, j, v, w, y**

Consonants: qu, x, z

1. 👄 Say each picture name. 2. 👂 Listen to the first and last sounds.
3. ✏️ Print **qu** or **z** if you hear those beginning sounds. Print **x** if you hear that ending sound.

Row 1: z _ _ _

1 Say the sound the letter or letters stand for.
2 Listen to that sound in each picture name.
3 Print the letter or letters to show where you hear that sound in the picture name.

qu		z		x		qu	
z		x		qu		z	
x		qu		z		x	
x		z		x		z	
x		qu		z		x	

12

1. 🗣 Say each picture name.
2. 👂 Listen to the first and last sounds.
3. ✏️ Print the letters that stand for the first and last sounds you hear.

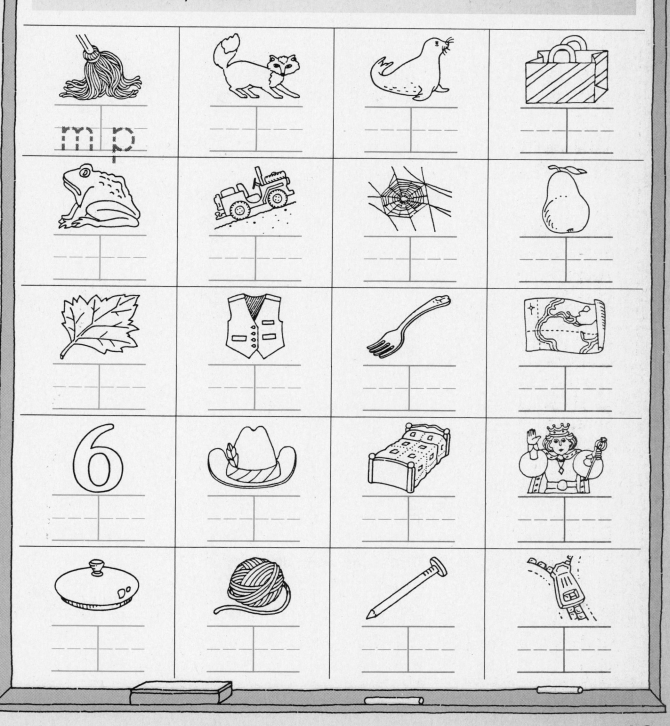

1 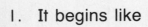 Read the clues below.
2 ✏ Print the word from the box that fits the clues.

had	box	dog	soap
from	miss	rain	cat

1. It begins like and ends like 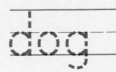 .   dog

2. It begins like and ends like .

3. It begins like and ends like .

4. It begins like and ends like .

5. It begins like and ends like .

6. It begins like and ends like .

7. It begins like and ends like  .

8. It begins like and ends like .

14

1 📖 Read each clue.   2 📖 Then read the word in the box.
3 ✏️ Change the underlined letter to make a new word
that fits the clue.

1. We can ride in this.

| bu_t_ |

bus

2. This pet was once a pup.

| _l_og |

3. You see me in the sky.

| _f_un |

4. This is made of tin.

| ca_t_ |

5. You play this.

| _n_ame |

6. This is on a tree.

| lea_p_ |

7. You can take a ride in this.

| _d_eep |

8. You can play ball with this.

| _h_at |

9. A pig sits in one of these.

| pe_t_ |

10. You can take a nap here.

| be_g_ |

b c d f g h j k l m n p q r s t v w x y z

Directions: Say the name of the picture. Listen to the first sound. Fill in the space next to the letter that stands for the first sound you hear.

Example

○ t
○ v
○ f

1. ○ p ○ b ○ d	2. ○ f ○ h ○ k	3. ○ l ○ z ○ s	4. ○ k ○ r ○ g
5. ○ d ○ n ○ p	6. ○ t ○ b ○ p	7. ○ s ○ c ○ b	8. ○ j ○ g ○ p
9. ○ s ○ r ○ h	10. ○ w ○ g ○ m	11. ○ m ○ d ○ b	12. ○ w ○ t ○ v
13. ○ n ○ m ○ k	14. ○ k ○ qu ○ t	15. ○ s ○ b ○ z	16. ○ l ○ f ○ t
17. ○ j ○ y ○ n	18. ○ m ○ s ○ n	19. ○ k ○ qu ○ n	20. ○ g ○ t ○ y

16

Short Vowels: a

1. 🗣 Say the sound of each letter as you trace the line.
2. 👂 Listen to the sounds of the letters as they blend together.
3. ✏ Draw a line from each word to its picture.

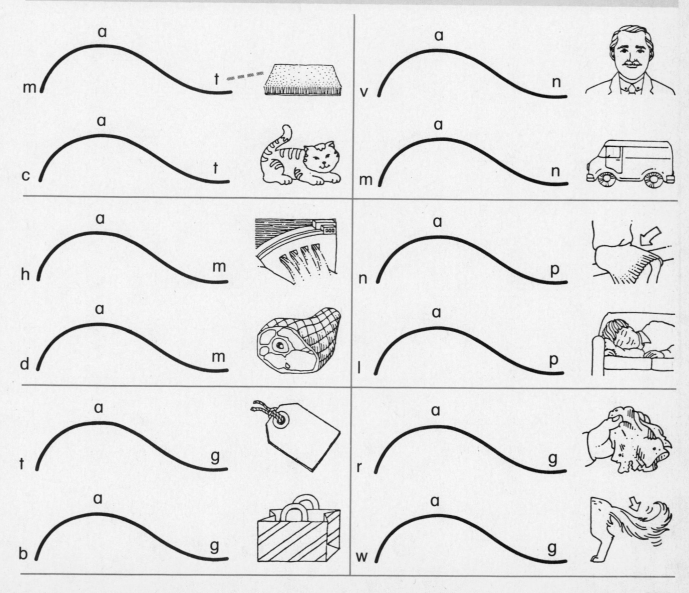

1 Say each picture name.
2 Listen for the short sound of **a**.
3 Print **a** if you hear the short sound of **a**.

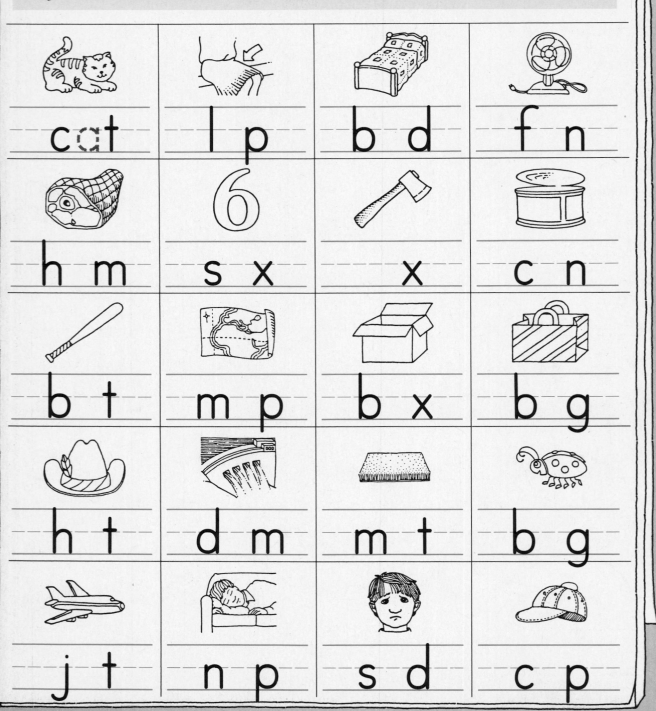

c a t	l __ p	b __ d	f __ n
h __ m	s __ x	__ x	c __ n
b __ t	m __ p	b __ x	b __ g
h __ t	d __ m	m __ t	b __ g
j __ t	n __ p	s __ d	c __ p

18

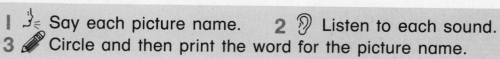

Short Vowels:
a

1 ✋ Say each picture name. 2 👂 Listen to each sound.
3 ✏️ Circle and then print the word for the picture name.

cab cap cat	rag ran rat	pan pad pat
cap		
bat bag bad	cab can cap	bad bag bat
map mad man	hat ham has	man map mad
tag tan tap	fat fad fan	cap cat can

Using the short sound of **a**

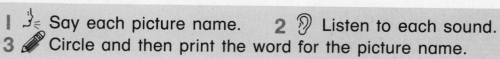

19

1 📖 Read each sentence.

2 ✏️ Print a word that rhymes with the underlined word.

Make the sentence tell about the picture.

1. The <u>cat</u> sat on a _mat_ .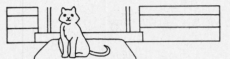

2. That <u>man</u> has a _____ .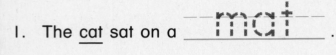

3. Put this <u>tag</u> on the _____ .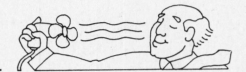

4. Is he <u>sad</u> or _____ ?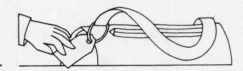

5. The cat took a <u>nap</u> on my _____ !

6. The <u>map</u> is on my _____ .

7. Gran has the <u>can</u> and a _____ .

8. What a <u>fat</u> _____ !

Short Vowels:
a

1 📖 Read the words.
2 ✏️ Make a sentence by printing the words in the right order.

1. is sad. Pam

Pam is sad.

2. mad. is Dan

_____

3. a Sam van. has

_____

4. cat fast. ran That

_____

5. a Pat sat on mat.

_____

6. has The man a map.

_____

7. a cap. Jan had tan

_____

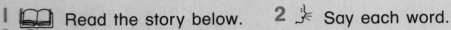

1 📖 Read the story below.   2 🏃 Say each word.

3 👂 Listen carefully for the short sound of **a**.

4 ✏️ Draw a line under each word with the short sound of **a**.

A tan hat ran at Dan.
Dan ran from that tan hat!
That tan hat ran at Pam.
Pam ran from that tan hat!

Dad looked at that tan hat.
"How can a hat do that?"
Dad had to have that hat!

Dad put that tan hat in his lap.
A cat ran from the hat.
That cat ran from the hat on Dad's lap!
That cat landed on the mat and sat.

1 📖 Read each question about the story.

2 ✏️ Fill in the space by the correct answer.

1. Dan ran from a
   ○ cat.
   ○ Dad.
   ● hat.
   ○ mat.

2. What did Dad put on his lap?
   ○ a lad
   ○ a mat
   ○ a tan cat
   ○ a hat

3. That cat sat on a
   ○ lap.
   ○ mat.
   ○ rat.
   ○ hat.

4. Which is the best title for this story?
   ○ "A Tan Hat"
   ○ "A Cat on a Mat"
   ○ "A Hat That Ran"
   ○ "Dan and Pam"

Short Vowels: i

1. Say the sound of each letter as you trace the line.
2. Listen to the sounds of the letters as they blend together.
3. Draw a line from each word to its picture.

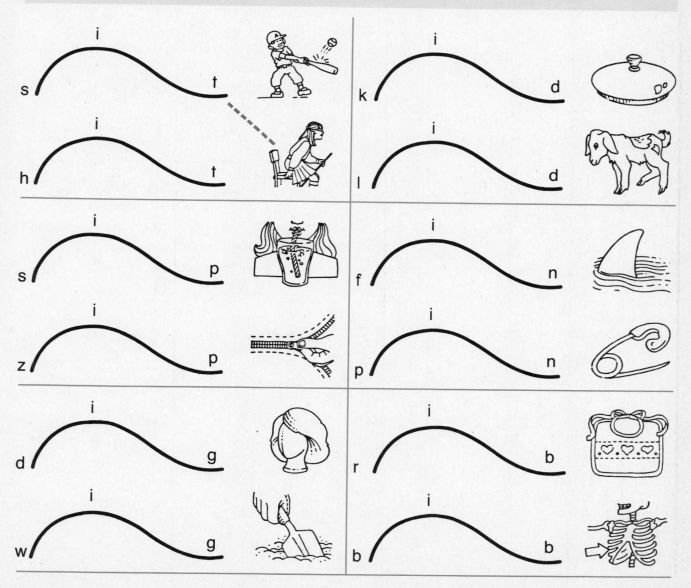

1 🗣 Say each picture name.
2 👂 Listen for the short sound of **i**.
3 ✏ Print **i** if you hear the short sound of **i**.
4 ✏ Then go back and print **a** if you hear the short sound of **a**.

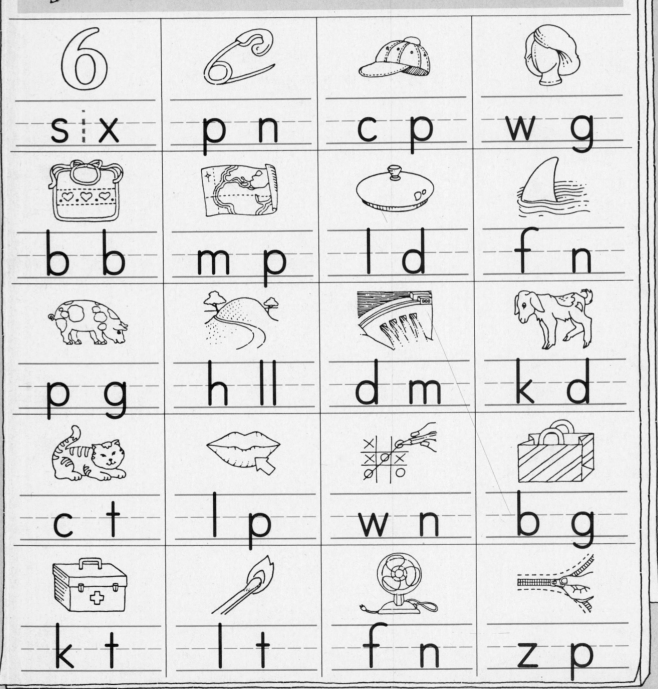

s i x   p __ n   c __ p   w __ g

b __ b   m __ p   l __ d   f __ n

p __ g   h __ l l   d __ m   k __ d

c __ t   l __ p   w __ n   b __ g

k __ t   l __ t   f __ n   z __ p

1 🗣 Say each picture name.   2 👂 Listen to each sound.
3 ✏ Circle and then print the word for the picture name.

	(pin)		sit		bit
	pit		sip		bib
	pan		six		bat

pin

	lit		wig		lad
	lap		win		lid
	lip		wag		lip

	pit		fit		dip
	pin		fin		did
	pig		fan		dig

	rib		tin		hat
	rid		tip		hit
	rip		tap		hid

1 📖 Read each sentence.
2 ✏️ Print a word that rhymes with the underlined word.
Make the sentence tell about the picture.

1. This <u>wig</u> is too _big_ .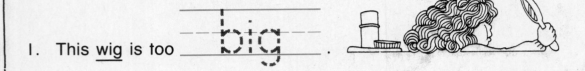

2. He can <u>fix</u> all _____ .

3. Jill <u>will</u> go to the top of the _____ .

4. This <u>pig</u> likes to _____ .

5. The <u>fish</u> is on the _____ .

6. Bill <u>hid</u> the _____ .

7. You get a <u>pin</u> if you _____ .

8. It will not <u>fit</u> in the _____ .

1 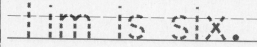 Read the words.
2 ✏ Make a sentence by printing the words in the right order.

1. is   six.   Tim

Tim is six.

2. hat.   hid   Liz   his

3. Pam   dish?   this   Can   fix

4. fish   His   big.   is

5. pig   Jim.   sits   The   with

6. fit   the   wig   Kim?   Did

7. mitt   not   This   fit.   will

Using language arts; writing sentences with words with the short sound of i

1 📖 Read the story below.   2 🎵 Say each word.
3 👂 Listen carefully for the short sound of **i**.
4 ✏️ Draw a line under each word with the short sound of **i**.

Bigs is a pig.
Will this pig play?
No, this pig will not play.
Is this pig sick?
No, this pig is not sick.
This pig is sad.

Bigs misses his pal Kim.
Kim misses him, too.
Kim is on a trip.
When Kim comes back,
Bigs will give her a big kiss.
Kim will wish she was still on her trip!

1 📖 Read each question about the story.
2 ✏️ Fill in the space by the correct answer.

1. Who is on a trip?
   ● Kim
   ○ a pig
   ○ Bigs
   ○ Miss

2. Who is Bigs?
   ○ a pal
   ○ Kim
   ○ a pig
   ○ a trip

3. What will Bigs give Kim?
   ○ a kiss
   ○ a trip
   ○ a pal
   ○ a pig

4. Which is the best title for this story?
   ○ "The Big Trip"
   ○ "Kim's Pig"
   ○ "Bigs' Trip"
   ○ "The Missing Pig"

1 📖 Read the underlined word and change the vowel sound to make the word that names the picture.
2 ✏️ Print the new word on the line.

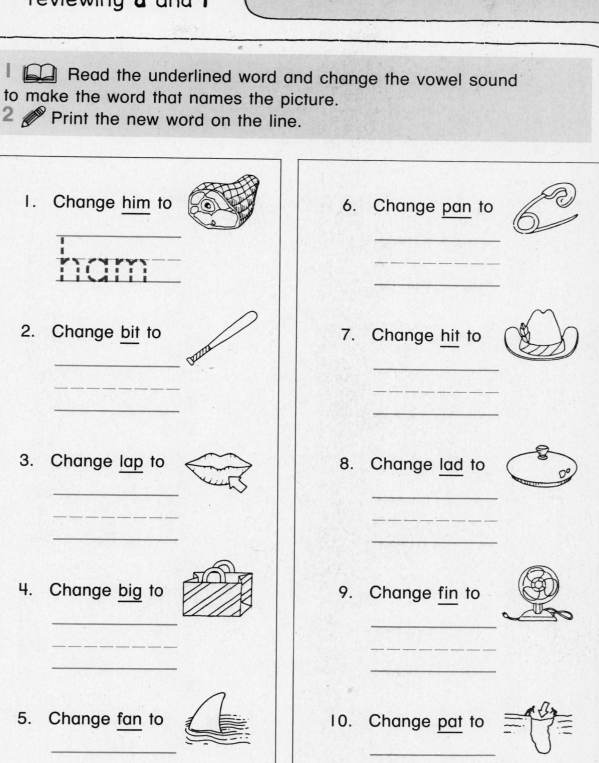

1. Change <u>him</u> to

ham

2. Change <u>bit</u> to

3. Change <u>lap</u> to

4. Change <u>big</u> to

5. Change <u>fan</u> to

6. Change <u>pan</u> to

7. Change <u>hit</u> to

8. Change <u>lad</u> to

9. Change <u>fin</u> to

10. Change <u>pat</u> to

Short Vowels:

o

1 Say the sound of each letter as you trace the line.
2 Listen to the sounds of the letters as they blend together.
3 Draw a line from each word to its picture.

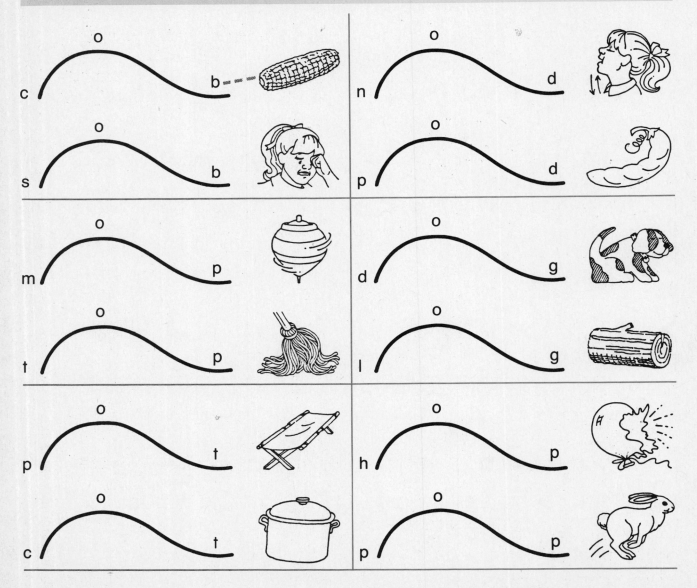

o
c   b

o
s   b

o
m   p

o
t   p

o
p   t

o
c   t

o
n   d

o
p   d

o
d   g

o
l   g

o
h   p

o
p   p

Introducing the short sound of o; blending words

Short Vowels:
o

1 ✍ Say each picture name. 2 👂 Listen for the short sound of **o**.
3 ✏️ Print **o** if you hear the short sound of **o**.
4 ✍ Then go back and print the letters for the other short vowel sounds you hear.

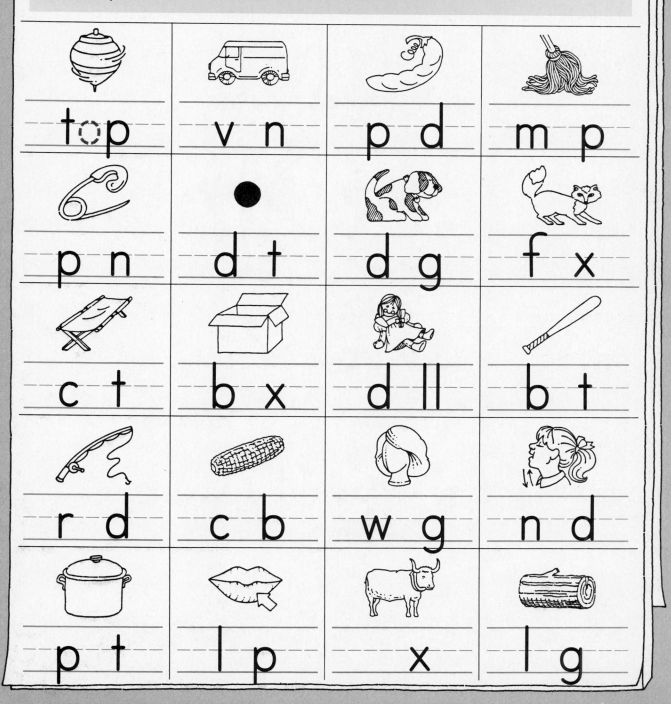

t**o**p	v__n	p__d	m__p
p__n	d__t	d__g	f__x
c__t	b__x	d__ll	b__t
r__d	c__b	w__g	n__d
p__t	l__p	__x	l__g

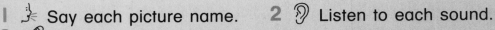

1 🗣 Say each picture name.   2 👂 Listen to each sound.
3 ✏️ Circle and then print the word for the picture name.

	dig		rid		cob
	(dog)		rot		cot
	dot		rod		cat
	dog				

	dot		hot		top
●	dig		hop		tip
	dog		hog		tap

	map		pod		fix
	mob		pad		fog
	mop		pot		fox

	cab		box		pot
	cot		bob		pod
	cob		bog		pop

Using the short sound of **o**

1 📖 Read each sentence.
2 ✏️ Print a word that rhymes with the underlined word.
Make the sentence tell about the picture.

1. The <u>dog</u> is on a ___log___ .

2. <u>Bob</u> will do a good _____ .

3. A <u>fox</u> is in the _____ .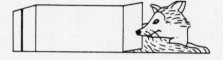

4. I can <u>hop</u> with the _____ .

5. <u>Stop</u> when you get to the _____ .

6. The man had a <u>dog</u> and a _____ .

7. Dot <u>got</u> too _____ .

8. Roz will <u>jog</u> in the _____ .

Using language arts; rhyming words; using context clues to select words with the short sound of o

Short Vowels:
o

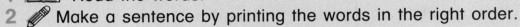

1 📖 Read the words.
2 ✏️ Make a sentence by printing the words in the right order.

1. got   Bob   lost.

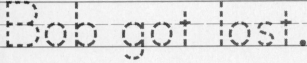

2. hot?   too   Is   Ron

_____

3. Tom   hop?   Can

_____

4. not   ox   did   stop.   The

_____

5. logs?   on   frogs   hop   Can

_____

6. will   the   Dot   mop   shop.   not

_____

7. Mom   drop   hot   pot?   the   Did

_____

Using language arts; writing sentences with words with the short sound of **o**

1 📖 Read the story below. 2 🎵 Say each word.
3 👂 Listen carefully for the short sound of **o**.
4 ✏️ Draw a line under each word with the short sound of **o**.

<u>Spots</u> is a <u>frog</u>.
It hops a lot.
It hops on a log.
Then it hops on Bob's cot.

Bob is not happy with Spots on his cot.
He will get Spots to hop into a box.
That will get Spots off his cot.

Bob gets a box.
He puts the box by the cot.
But that frog did not hop into the box.
No, Spots hopped on Bob!

1 📖 Read each question about the story.
2 ✏️ Fill in the space by the correct answer.

1. Spots is a
    ○ pal.
    ○ cot.
    ● frog.
    ○ Bob.

2. What did Bob get?
    ○ a top
    ○ a box
    ○ a cot
    ○ a hop

3. Spots did not hop
    ○ on a log.
    ○ into a box.
    ○ on a cot.
    ○ on Bob.

4. Which is the best title for this story?
    ○ "A Hop on a Cot"
    ○ "Bob Hops"
    ○ "A Log and a Box"
    ○ "A Frog on a Log"

1 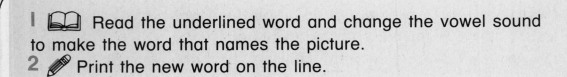 Read the underlined word and change the vowel sound
to make the word that names the picture.
2 ✏ Print the new word on the line.

1. Change <u>tap</u> to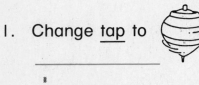

top

2. Change <u>fix</u> to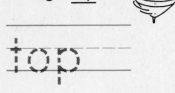

_____

3. Change <u>hot</u> to

_____

4. Change <u>rob</u> to

_____

5. Change <u>cob</u> to

6. Change <u>pad</u> to

_____

7. Change <u>dig</u> to

_____

8. Change <u>lad</u> to

_____

9. Change <u>pat</u> to

_____

10. Change <u>mop</u> to

_____

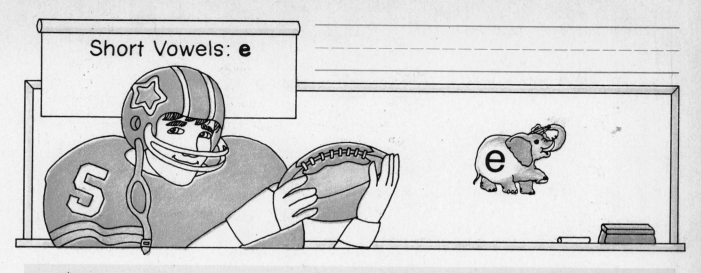

Short Vowels: **e**

1. 🗣 Say the sound of each letter as you trace the line.
2. 👂 Listen to the sounds of the letters as they blend together.
3. ✏ Draw a line from each word to its picture.

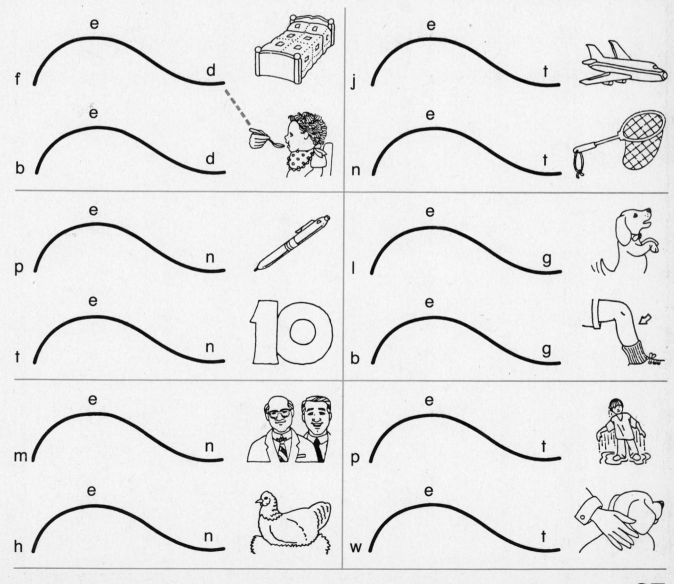

1 🗣 Say each picture name.   2 👂 Listen for the short sound of **e**.
3 ✏️ Print **e** if you hear the short sound of **e**.
4 ✎ Then go back and print the letters for the other short vowel sounds you hear.

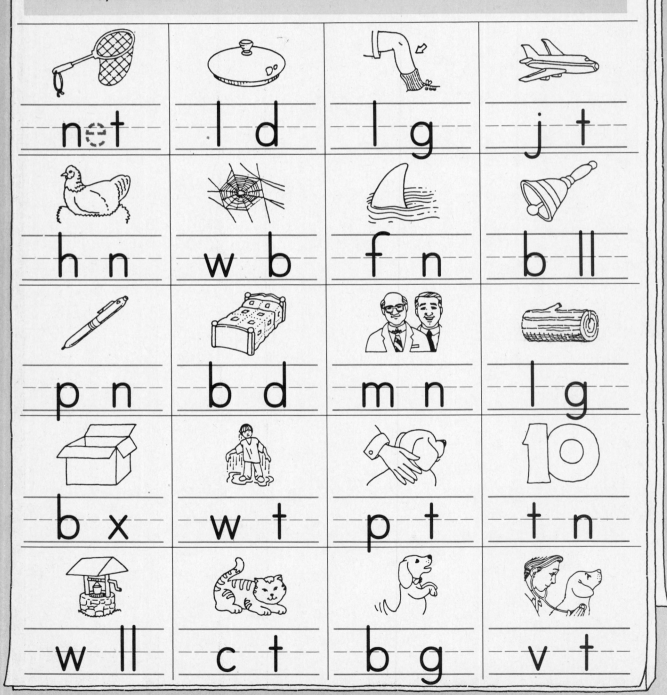

n e t	l _ d	l _ g	j _ t
h _ n	w _ b	f _ n	b _ ll
p _ n	b _ d	m _ n	l _ g
b _ x	w _ t	p _ t	t _ n
w _ ll	c _ t	b _ g	v _ t

Short Vowels: e

1. 👄 Say each picture name.　2. 👂 Listen to each sound.
3. ✏️ Circle and then print the word for the picture name.

(bed) / bit / bad	met / not / net	ten / tan / tin
bed		
jot / jet / jam	lag / log / leg	ham / hen / him
bag / beg / big	men / man / met	wed / web / wet
pen / pin / pan	wet / web / wed	pet / pit / pot

Using the short sound of **e**

39

Short Vowels:
e

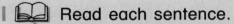

1 📖 Read each sentence.
2 ✏️ Print a word that rhymes with the underlined word.
Make the sentence tell about the picture.

1. We <u>fed</u> the baby in her bed .

2. Here are <u>ten</u> _____ .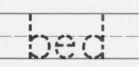

3. The hen <u>fell</u> in the _____ .

4. They <u>met</u> on a _____ .

5. The <u>hen</u> is in a _____ .

6. Mom <u>let</u> me get a _____ .

7. Did you <u>sell</u> the _____ ?

8. I will <u>get</u> ready with the _____ .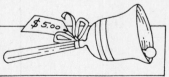

40   Using language arts; rhyming words; using context clues to select words with the short sound of **e**

1 📖 Read the words.
2 ✏ Make a sentence by printing the words in the right order.

1. Was wet? net the

Was the net wet?

2. We Ben. met with

3. bells? sell Deb Will

4. fed vet her pet. The

5. will get hen wet. That

6. Bev a dress. has red

7. the Will get men? Fred

1 📖 Read the story below. 　　2 🎙 Say each word.
3 👂 Listen carefully for the short sound of **e**.
4 ✏️ Draw a line under each word with the short sound of **e**.

Len has a red hen. Len's hen is a pet.
What can Len do with a pet hen?
Len can tell the hen to sit.
Len can tell the hen to beg.
Len can pat the red hen.

One day, Len took the hen to the vet.
"My hen is not well," said Len.
"My hen has a bad leg."
The vet set the hen's leg.
"Let the hen rest," said the vet.
"You rest in this nest," said Len.
"You are the best pet. You will get well."

1 📖 Read each question about the story.
2 ✏️ Fill in the space by the correct answer.

1. The hen is Len's
   ○ red.
   ● pet.
   ○ vet.
   ○ bed.

2. The hen had a bad
   ○ vet.
   ○ nest.
   ○ leg.
   ○ rest.

3. Len took the hen to the
   ○ pet.
   ○ leg.
   ○ red.
   ○ vet.

4. Which is the best title for this story?
   ○ "Len's Hen"
   ○ "The Bad Hen"
   ○ "The Hen's Vet"
   ○ "The Hen's Rest"

Using language arts; reading a story with words with the short sound of **e**; story comprehension

1 📖 Read the underlined word and change the vowel sound
to make the word that names the picture.
2 ✏️ Print the new word on the line.

1. Change <u>log</u> to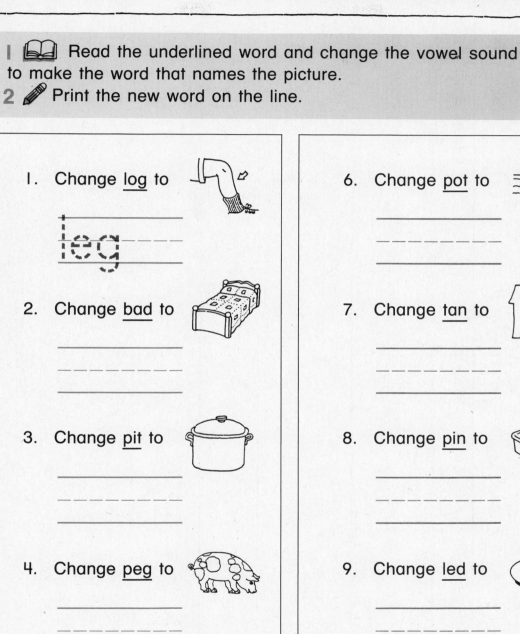

   leg

2. Change <u>bad</u> to

3. Change <u>pit</u> to

4. Change <u>peg</u> to

5. Change <u>cat</u> to

6. Change <u>pot</u> to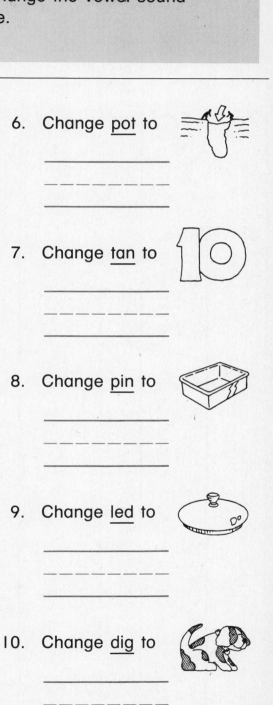

7. Change <u>tan</u> to

8. Change <u>pin</u> to

9. Change <u>led</u> to

10. Change <u>dig</u> to

Short Vowels:
u

1. Say the sound of each letter as you trace the line.
2. Listen to the sounds of the letters as they blend together.
3. Draw a line from each word to its picture.

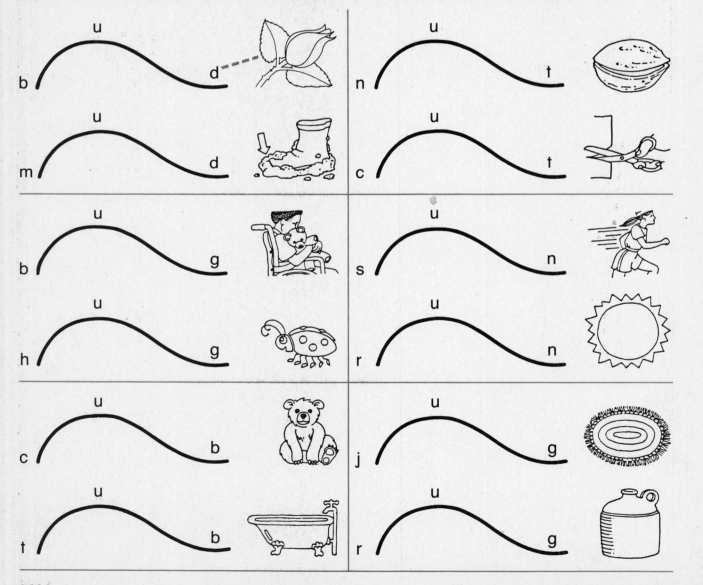

b u d

m u d

b u g

h u g

c u b

t u b

n u t

c u t

s u n

r u n

j u g

r u g

Introducing the short sound of **u**; blending words

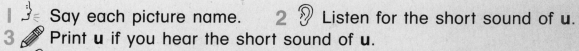

1 Say each picture name.   2 Listen for the short sound of **u**.
3 Print **u** if you hear the short sound of **u**.
4 Then go back and print the letters for the other short vowel
sounds you hear.

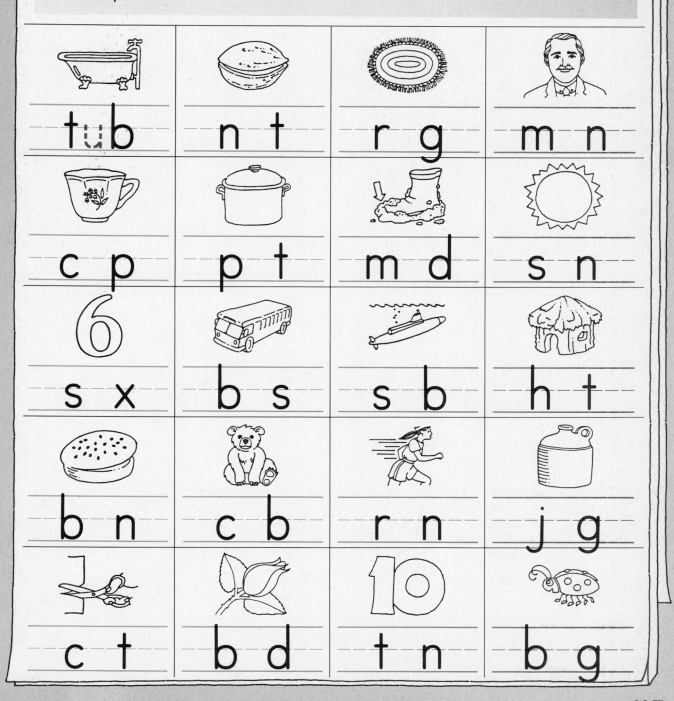

t u b	n t	r g	m n
c p	p t	m d	s n
s x	b s	s b	h t
b n	c b	r n	j g
c t	b d	t n	b g

1 ✎ Say each picture name.   2 👂 Listen to each sound.
3 ✏ Circle and then print the word for the picture name.

 cap (cup) cut	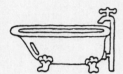 tub tab tug	 mad mug mud
not nut net	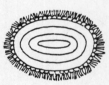 pop pep pup	 rug rag rub
jug jig rug	 bud bus bun	 hat hit hut
 sob sub sun	 ban bin bun	 run rub rug

46

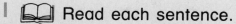

1 📖 Read each sentence.
2 ✏️ Print a word that rhymes with the underlined word.
Make the sentence tell about the picture.

1. The <u>cub</u> is in the ___tub___.

2. The dog will <u>tug</u> on the _____.

3. The <u>bud</u> fell in the _____.

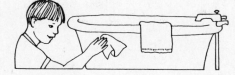

4. He will <u>rub</u> the _____.

5. I can <u>run</u> in the _____.

6. I fed the <u>pup</u> in a _____.

7. <u>Gus</u> will get on a _____.

8. A <u>bug</u> is on the _____.

1 📖 Read the words.
2 ✏️ Make a sentence by printing the words in the right order.

1. nuts.   likes   Russ

Russ likes nuts.

2. Have   in   fun   sun.   the

3. the   buns   hot?   Are

4. for   runs   fun.   Pug

5. Lil's   pup   a   tug   rug?   Will

6. on   fuss   Gus   the   will   bus.

7. dug   dog   mud.   in   the   That

Using language arts; writing sentences with words with the short sound of **u**

1 📖 Read the story below.   2 🗣 Say each word.
3 👂 Listen carefully for the short sound of **u**.
4 ✏️ Draw a line under each word with the short sound of **u**.

Bud is a pup. Bud dug in the mud.
Bud dug up a cup that was in the mud.
Bud took the cup to Mom.
Bud got mud on the rug.

Mom got mad.
Mom set Bud in a tub with lots of suds.
She rubbed those suds on Bud.
Bud did not have fun.

Mom had Bud dry in the sun.
Mom gave the pup a hug.
She said, "You can run in the sun.
But keep that mud off my rug!"

1 📖 Read each question about the story.
2 ✏️ Fill in the space by the correct answer.

1. Bud is a
   ● pup.
   ○ tub.
   ○ Mom.
   ○ nut.

2. Where did Bud dig?
   ○ in the rug
   ○ in the cup
   ○ in the tub
   ○ in the mud

3. What did Mom do?
   ○ dug
   ○ rubbed Bud
   ○ set a tub in mud
   ○ ran

4. Which is the best title for this story?
   ○ "Mom's Rug"
   ○ "The Pup in the Mud"
   ○ "Bud's Cup"
   ○ "Mom's Mud"

Short Vowels: reviewing **a**, **e**, **i**, **o**, and **u**

1 📖 Read the underlined word and change the vowel sound to make the word that names the picture.
2 ✏️ Print the new word on the line.

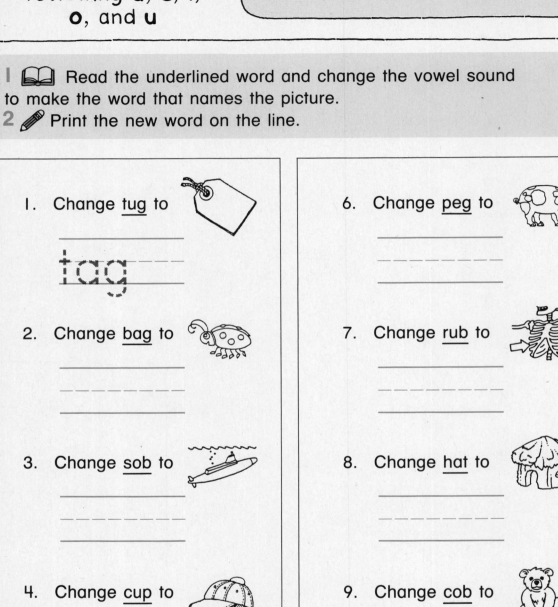

1. Change <u>tug</u> to

   tag

2. Change <u>bag</u> to

3. Change <u>sob</u> to

4. Change <u>cup</u> to

5. Change <u>nut</u> to

6. Change <u>peg</u> to

7. Change <u>rub</u> to

8. Change <u>hat</u> to

9. Change <u>cob</u> to

10. Change <u>mud</u> to

Unit Review: short vowels

1 Say each picture name.
2 Listen for the vowel sound.
3 Print the word for the picture name.

top

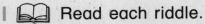

1 📖 Read each riddle.
2 ✏️ Circle the correct answer.
3 ✏️ Print the answer in a complete sentence.

1. I am on a fish. Am I a pin, (fin,) or fan?

A fin is on a fish.

2. You ride in me. Am I a bun, bat, or bus?

3. You can eat me. Am I a hit, ham, or hat?

4. I am on your face. Am I a lip, hip, or lap?

5. I can fly in the sky. Am I a jet, pig, or pet?

6. You can play tug with me. Am I a pot, pet, or top?

7. You can sleep on me. Am I a cot, cat, or nut?

1 📖 Read each silly question.
2 ✏️ Print **yes** or **no** to answer the question.

1. Can a fish get wet?

   yes

2. Is a can a pet?

   - - - - -

3. Can an egg be hot?

   - - - - -

4. Can a tub run up a big hill?

   - - - - -

5. Does a bug have legs?

   - - - - -

6. Can a dog sit on a log?

   - - - - -

1 📖 Read the words in the box.
2 ✏️ Use words from the box and your own words
to write silly questions of your own.

on	be	a	is	cub	box	ten	has	dig
cup	cot	men	can	pig	run	fox	bed
pat	six	sun	hop	get	rat	sit	tub

1. Can a box

2. - - - - -

3. - - - - -

a e i o u

Directions: Say each picture name. Listen to the vowel sound. Fill in the space next to the word for the picture name.

Example

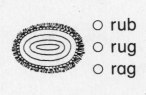

○ rub
○ rug
○ rag

1. ○ pan ○ pin ○ pen	**2.** ○ fin ○ fun ○ fan	**3.** ○ dug ○ dig ○ dog	**4.** ○ net ○ nut ○ not
5. ○ lad ○ lid ○ led	**6.** ○ pen ○ pan ○ pin	**7.** ○ him ○ ham ○ hum	**8.** ○ cup ○ cap ○ cot
9. ○ cub ○ cab ○ cob	**10.** ○ log ○ leg ○ lag	**11.** ○ pin ○ pan ○ pen	**12.** ○ cat ○ cut ○ cot
13. ○ hot ○ hit ○ hut	**14.** ○ big ○ bag ○ beg	**15.** ○ top ○ tap ○ tip	**16.** ○ not ○ net ○ nut
17. ○ pug ○ peg ○ pig	**18.** ○ rod ○ rid ○ red	**19.** ○ bad ○ bed ○ bud	**20.** ○ hat ○ hit ○ hot

Testing short vowel sounds; using an adapted standardized test format

Long Vowels: ā

1 Say each picture name.
2 Listen to the vowel sound.
3 Circle **ā** if you hear the long sound of **a**.
Circle **a** if you hear the short sound of **a**.

Long Vowels:
ā

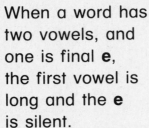

When a word has two vowels, and one is final **e**, the first vowel is long and the **e** is silent.

lāk¢

When two vowels are together, the first vowel is usually long and the second is silent.

nā/l

When **y** follows the vowel **a**, the **y** is silent and the **a** is long.

pāy

1 Print each word under its spelling pattern.
2 Mark the letters as shown.

sale	wait	may	paid	play	make	day	main
rain	lane	way	late	same	ray	mail	

_ā_¢ = ā

sāl¢

ā/ = ā

āy = ā

1 📖 Read each sentence.
2 ✏️ Print a word that rhymes with the underlined word.
Make the sentence tell about the picture.

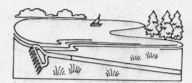

1. A <u>rake</u> is by the ___lake___ .

2. I <u>pay</u> for my meal every _____ .

3. The dog with the <u>mail</u> wags its _____ .

4. We were <u>late</u>, so they shut the _____ .

5. Jake <u>came</u> to the _____ .

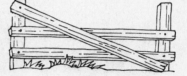

6. The <u>rail</u> needs a _____ .

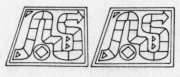

7. Each <u>game</u> is the _____ .

8. We rode the <u>train</u> in the _____ .

Long Vowels: ā

1 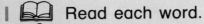 Read each word.
2 ✏ Make a sentence by printing the words in the right order.

1. pay   Can   for   Jay   the   nails?

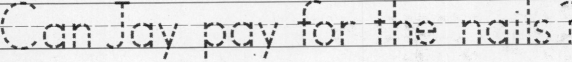

Can Jay pay for the nails?

2. mail   Is   late?   this

3. plays   with   Dale   his   cat.

4. will   Dad   bay.   the   sail   on

5. can   rake   Jake   hay.   the

6. wait   Did   in   rain?   Jane   the

7. will   play   Gail   lake.   the   by

Using language arts; writing sentences with words with the long sound of a

1 📖 Read the story below.   2 🗣 Say each word.
3 👂 Listen carefully for the long sound of **a**.
4 ✏️ Draw a line under each word with the long sound of **a**.

Gail can make a plate out of clay.
First she sits at a wheel.
She puts the clay on top.
She uses her toe to make the wheel
go around.
She makes the clay into a round shape.
Then she takes the clay off the wheel.
She bakes the clay plate.
After the plate bakes, she puts a gray
glaze on it.
Then she bakes the plate again.

1 📖 Read each question about the story.
2 ✏️ Fill in the space by the correct answer.

1. What does Gail use to make a plate?
   ○ gray glaze
   ● clay
   ○ bake
   ○ her toe

2. What does the plate look like?
   ○ a round shape
   ○ a rake
   ○ a pail
   ○ a sail

3. What does Gail do to the clay plate?
   ○ plays with it
   ○ bakes it
   ○ bites it
   ○ takes it

4. Which is the best title for this story?
   ○ "Gail Has a Bad Day"
   ○ "Gail Makes a Clay Plate"
   ○ "Gail Can Play"
   ○ "Gail's Clay"

Long Vowels:
ī

1. 🎋 Say each picture name.
2. 👂 Listen to the vowel sound.
3. ✏️ Circle ī if you hear the long sound of **i**.

Circle **i** if you hear the short sound of **i**.

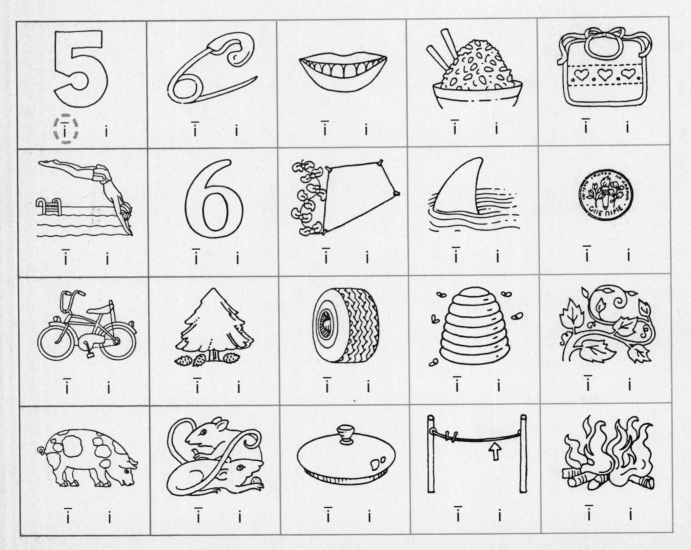

Introducing the long sound of **i**

Long Vowels:
ī

When a word has two vowels, and one is final **e**, the first vowel is long and the **e** is silent.

bīke̸

When two vowels are together, the first vowel is usually long and the second is silent.

tīe̸

1 🖉 Print each word under its spelling pattern.
2 🖉 Mark the letters as shown.

kite	lie	nine	die	hide
pie	lime	tie	die	tide

_ ī _ e̸ = ī   _ ī e̸ = ī

kīte̸

1. 📖 Read each sentence.
2. ✏️ Print a word that rhymes with the underlined word.
Make the sentence tell about the picture.

1. All <u>five</u> will __dive__ .

2. We will hike in a <u>file</u> for one _____ .

3. He got his <u>tie</u> in the _____ .

4. They put the <u>tile</u> in a _____ .

5. There are two <u>lines</u> of _____ .

6. Bill can fly a <u>white</u> _____ .

7. What a <u>fine</u> _____ this is!

8. Kim can buy a <u>lime</u> for a _____ .

1 📖 Read each word.
2 ✏️ Make a sentence by printing the words in the right order.

1. tie. can a Gail make

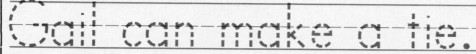
Gail can make a tie.

2. a bike? ride Can Mike

3. away. is miles nine lake The

4. kite Her into the went wire.

5. for It days. rained five

6. Blake will lie. tell not a

7. that Miles Did wade in lake?

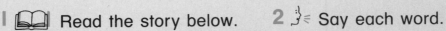

1  Read the story below. 2 Say each word.
3 Listen carefully for the long sound of **i**.
4 Draw a line under each word with the long sound of **i**.

<u>Mike</u> and Kim <u>ride</u> their <u>bikes</u>.
They ride on the right side of the road.
They ride under tall pines.
They ride miles to Tom's home.
Then they stop to help Tom take
grapes off his vines.
The grapes are fat and fine.
After a while, it is time to go.
Mike and Kim have nine piles
of grapes.
They tie the grapes on their bikes
and ride home.

1 Read each question about the story.
2 Fill in the space by the correct answer.

1. Where did Mike and Kim ride?
   ● on the right side
     of the road
   ○ on a path
   ○ under the vines
   ○ on a vine

2. Where were the grapes?
   ○ on the pines
   ○ on the road
   ○ at Mike's house
   ○ on the vines

3. How many grapes did Mike and Kim have?
   ○ nine
   ○ nine piles
   ○ miles
   ○ a while

4. Which is the best title for this story?
   ○ "The Tall Pines"
   ○ "Mike and Kim's Ride"
   ○ "Nine Vines"
   ○ "Kim's Bike"

Long Vowels:
reviewing ā and ī

1 📖 Read each sentence.
2 ✏️ Circle the words that make sense in the sentence.

1. There are ~~line~~ (nine) bats in that ~~save~~ (cave).

2. Mike will hide / ride his bike / hike to the lake.

3. May / Say I buy that blue lie / tie ?

4. The fish ate the wait / bait off the line / dine .

5. There is a fine / vine by our gate / date .

6. The mail / pail came date / late .

7. Use some cape / tape to fix your kite / bite .

8. There is a nail / rail in that tail / pail .

9. What is the same / name of his wife / life ?

10. We will dive / hive into the lake / rake .

Long Vowels: ō

1. 🗣 Say each picture name.
2. 👂 Listen to the vowel sound.
3. ✏️ Circle ō if you hear the long sound of o.

Circle o if you hear the short sound of o.

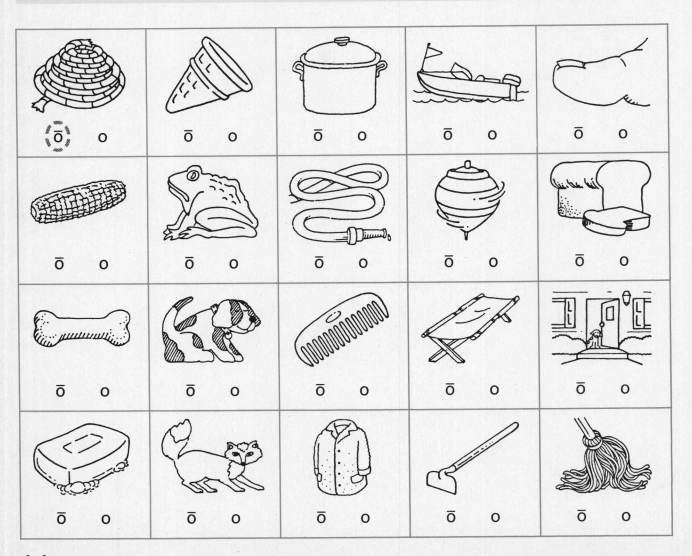

ō	o	ō	o	ō	o	ō	o	ō	o
ō	o	ō	o	ō	o	ō	o	ō	o
ō	o	ō	o	ō	o	ō	o	ō	o
ō	o	ō	o	ō	o	ō	o	ō	o

Introducing the long sound of **o**

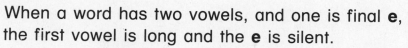

Long Vowels: ō

When a word has two vowels, and one is final **e**, the first vowel is long and the **e** is silent.

rōbé

When two vowels are together, the first vowel is usually long and the second is silent.

bōát    hōé

1 ✏ Print each word under its spelling pattern.
2 ✏ Mark the letters as shown.

goat	toe	toad	bone	hoe	soap	Joe	rope
Joan	hole	rose	doe	stove	loaf	foe	

 ōá = ō   ō_é = ō   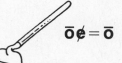 ōé = ō

gōát

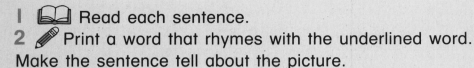

1 📖 Read each sentence.
2 ✏️ Print a word that rhymes with the underlined word.
Make the sentence tell about the picture.

1. The <u>mole</u> lives in a ___hole___ .

2. I <u>hope</u> you find your _____ .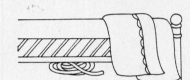

3. You smell a <u>rose</u> with your _____ .

4. Get that <u>toad</u> out of the _____ !

5. Do not hit your <u>toe</u> with the _____ !

6. Dig a <u>hole</u> for the _____ .

7. Joe gives <u>oats</u> to the _____ .

8. <u>Joan</u> will _____ her bike.

1 📖 Read each word.
2 ✏️ Make a sentence by printing the words in the right order.

1. gave   She   Joan   rose.   a

She gave Joan a rose.

2. Rose   go   Did   cove?   the   to

3. boat   not   That   float.   will

4. jokes.   likes   tell   Mike   to

5. put   Joe   mail.   a   in   the   note

6. soak   in   the   He   robe   soap.   will

7. rode   Zoe   on   home   her   bike.

1 📖 Read the story below.   2 🏃 Say each word.
3 👂 Listen carefully for the long sound of **o**.
4 ✏️ Draw a line under each word with the long sound of **o**.

One fine day, <u>Rose</u> and <u>Joe</u> <u>drove</u> to the <u>cove</u>.
They went for a walk around the cove.
They found shells, stones, and fish bones.
They found an old pail with a hole in it.
Rose and Joe put on their coats when they got cold.
Then they drove home.
They hope to take a ride to the cove again.

1 📖 Read each question about the story.
2 ✏️ Fill in the space by the correct answer.

1. Who drove to the cove?
   ● Rose and Joe
   ○ Rose
   ○ Joe
   ○ Mom

3. What did they do when they got cold?
   ○ They got old.
   ○ They put on coats.
   ○ They walked around the cove.
   ○ They made a fire.

2. What did they do first?
   ○ They drove home.
   ○ They went for a walk around the cove.
   ○ They put on their coats.
   ○ They found a pail.

4. Which is the best title for this story?
   ○ "A Day at the Cove"
   ○ "The Old Pail"
   ○ "Joe and Rose Get Cold"
   ○ "Stones and Fish Bones"

Using language arts; reading a story with words with the long sound of **o**; story comprehension

Long Vowels:
reviewing ā, ī,
and ō

1 📖 Read each sentence.
2 ✏️ Circle the words that make sense in the sentence.

1. We saw nine red (boats) / goats on the (lake) / rake .

2. Wipe / Ripe the soap / soak off the plate.

3. The hole / mole likes to hide / ride when it rains.

4. Joe / Toe will pay for that tie / die .

5. The nail made a pole / hole in the tire / fire .

6. My kite has a rail / tail made of rope / hope .

7. Jane paid a time / dime for her pet toad / load .

8. I rode / rope my bike in the main / rain .

9. We will hive / hike on the old roam / road ?

10. I hope / rope the mail / pail comes before five.

Reviewing the long sounds of **a**, **i**, and **o**

71

Long Vowels: ē

1. 👂 Say each picture name.
2. 👂 Listen to the vowel sound.
3. ✏️ Circle ē if you hear the long sound of **e**.

Circle **e** if you hear the short sound of **e**.

ⓔ e	ē e	ē e	ē e	ē e
ē e	ē e	ē e	ē e	ē e
ē e	ē e	ē e	ē e	ē e
ē e	ē e	ē e	ē e	ē e

72

When two vowels are together, the first vowel is usually long and the second is silent.

fēę̸t

sēą̸l

1 Print each word under its spelling pattern.
2 Mark the letters as shown.

| bee | meat | tree | weep | team |
| leak | need | tea | eat | teeth |

    ēę̸ = ē

bēę̸

ēą̸ = ē

1 📖 Read each sentence.
2 ✏️ Print a word that rhymes with the underlined word.
Make the sentence tell about the picture.

1. Dean had <u>tea</u> by the _____ sea _____ .

2. Jean said, "I <u>see</u> a fine pine _____ ."

3. Bev cut the <u>wheat</u> in the _____ .

4. Dave's <u>jeep</u> gave a big _____ .

5. Len just got <u>weeds</u> from his _____ .

6. Joan put the <u>beans</u> in her _____ .

7. Can mom <u>reach</u> that big _____ ?

8. Jill looks so <u>neat</u> on that _____ .

Using language arts; rhyming words; using sentence context to select words with the long sound of **e**

Long Vowels: ē

1 📖 Read each word.
2 ✏️ Make a sentence by printing the words in the right order.

1. Will   the   feed   Jean   goat?

Will Jean feed the goat?

2. Lee   like   Does   meat?   that

_____

_____

3. team   The   each   meets   week.

_____

_____

4. sleep?   Pete   need   to   Did

_____

_____

5. We   beach.   at   the   meet   will

_____

_____

6. see   Do   big   you   trees?   the

_____

_____

7. eat   Dee   a   will   beet.   red

_____

_____

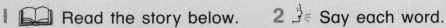

1 📖 Read the story below.   2 🗣 Say each word.
3 👂 Listen carefully for the long sound of **e**.
4 ✏️ Draw a line under each word with the long sound of **e**.

Bea has three peach trees.
These trees have fine green leaves.
They have lots of fat peaches.
Each peach smells sweet.
Each has fuzz on its skin.

There are lots of ways to eat peaches.
Bea likes to peel them and eat them
with cream.
Peaches and cream make a real treat.
Bea says she could eat a peach
at each meal!

1 📖 Read each question about the story.
2 ✏️ Fill in the space by the correct answer.

1. How many peach trees does
   Bea have?
   ● three
   ○ lots
   ○ one
   ○ a team

2. The peach tree leaves are
   ○ gray.
   ○ sweet.
   ○ neat.
   ○ green.

3. What does Bea like with her
   peaches?
   ○ leaves
   ○ cream
   ○ meat
   ○ peel

4. Which is the best title for this
   story?
   ○ "Bea Has a Meal"
   ○ "A Peach Is Fuzzy"
   ○ "Bea and the Peaches"
   ○ "Three Trees"

Long Vowels: reviewing ā, ē, ī, and ō

1 📖 Read each sentence.
2 ✏️ Circle the words that make sense in the sentence.

1. We ~~seed~~ (need) a new ~~bake~~ (rake) and hoe.

2. Our team / tear won the game by one foal / goal .

3. I hope / rope the mail comes before tree / three .

4. We will eat green jeans / beans this week / peek .

5. Please leave / leak a note / vote if you go out.

6. We will drive to the cove / rove in the jeep / peep .

7. We will hike up the toad / road through the leaves / weaves .

8. I cut my peel / heel on a nail / mail .

9. Please shut the gate / late when you lean / leave .

10. The dog will hide / ride its bone / lone by the tree.

Long Vowels: ū

1. 🗣 Say each picture name.
2. 👂 Listen to the vowel sound.
3. ✏️ Circle **ū** if you hear the long sound of **u**.

Circle **u** if you hear the short sound of **u**.

78

Long Vowels:
ū

When a word has two vowels, and one is final **e**, the first vowel is long and the **e** is silent.

mūl¢

When two vowels are together, the first vowel is usually long and the second is silent.

glū¢

1 🖉 Print each word under its spelling pattern.
2 🖉 Mark the letters as shown.

rule	due	cue	cube	tune
blue	true	flute	fuse	Sue

 _ū_¢ = ū

rūl¢

 _ū¢ = ū

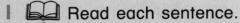

1 📖 Read each sentence.
2 ✏️ Print a word that rhymes with the underlined word.
Make the sentence tell about the picture.

1. Jean is <u>due</u> to find a ___clue___ .

2. Dad made a <u>rule</u> about that _____ .

3. Little <u>Sue</u> must not use _____ .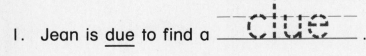

4. Is a <u>tube</u> the same as a _____ ?

5. Mom had to <u>use</u> a new _____ .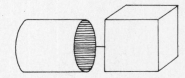

6. <u>June</u> sat on the _____ .

7. Is it <u>true</u> that the paint is _____ ?

8. Jake looks so <u>cute</u> with that _____ .

Long Vowels:
ū

1 📖 Read each word.
2 ✏️ Make a sentence by printing the words in the right order.

1. sun   is   The   hot   June.   in

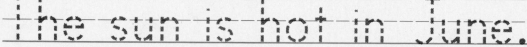
The sun is hot in June.

2. Can   that   use   Sue   glue?

_____

_____

3. rule?   Is   true   that   a

_____

_____

4. has   Jud   cube.   a   blue

_____

_____

5. is   fun   It   to   sun   on   a   dune.

_____

_____

6. use   a   fuse.   new   Dad   had   to

_____

_____

7. Duke   mule.   cute   has   a

_____

_____

1 📖 Read the story below.　　2 🗣 Say each word.
3 👂 Listen carefully for the long sound of **u**.
4 ✏️ Draw a line under each word with the long sound of **u**.

It was a pretty day in June.
Sue and her Dad were going to the dunes.
They drove in a blue jeep.
They called it the Dune Bug.

There were rules for going to the dunes.
Sue read the rules to her Dad.
You could not drive on the dunes.

Sue asked her Dad about the rules.
He said it was bad to use the dunes as a road.
Sue said, "I know that is true."

Sue and her Dad were happy to go by the rules.
They hummed a tune as they drove along.

1 📖 Read each question about the story.
2 ✏️ Fill in the space by the correct answer.

1. Sue and Dad went to the dunes
   ○ in May.
   ● in June.
   ○ at three.
   ○ at nine.

3. What did the rules say?
   ○ to go to the dunes
   ○ to drive on the dunes
   ○ not to drive on the dunes
   ○ to hum a tune

2. What did they call the jeep?
   ○ the Blue Bug
   ○ the Dune Jeep
   ○ the Blue Jeep
   ○ the Dune Bug

4. Which is the best title for this story?
   ○ "The Dune Bug"
   ○ "A Day at the Dunes"
   ○ "A Day in June"
   ○ "Rules for a Jeep"

1 📖 Read each sentence.
2 ✏️ Circle the words that make sense in the sentence.

1. Jake played a June
   (tune) on his (flute)
   cute .

2. The mail clue
   fail is due soon.

3. Duke ate prunes real
   tunes with his meal .

4. Is it true blue
   Sue a rose can be clue ?

5. May Joan fine goal
   ride down your road ?

6. Dad likes to use tie
   fuse this die .

7. June tune
   Fuse will hum a dune .

8. That role deep
   mole dug a leap hole.

9. Sue looks so cube day
   cute this say .

10. Can Luke use wire
    fuse coal in the fire ?

1 Say each picture name. 2 Listen to the vowel sound.
3 Print the word for the picture name.

nail

Unit review: spelling words with long vowel sounds

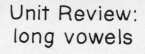

1 📖 Read the words in the box. 2 📖 Read each clue.
3 ✏️ Print the correct word in the puzzle.

| toe | blue | hay | flute | sleep | cube |
| pine | coat | hole | tail | pane | tie | seal |

ACROSS

2. You put this on when you are cold.
4. Mules eat this.
5. Our flag is red, white, and _____.
7. You can wash a _____ of glass.
8. You do this when you take a nap.
9. You can use a rope to do this.

DOWN

1. You can stub this.
2. This shape has six sides.
3. A dog wags this.
4. You can dig one of these.
6. You can use this to play a tune.
7. This tree stays green all year.
8. This can dive in the sea.

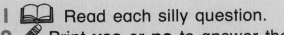

1 Read each silly question.
2 ✏️ Print **yes** or **no** to answer the question.

1. Can a bee make a hive?

   yes

2. Can glue come in a tube?

3. Does a toad have a tail?

4. Can you read when you doze?

5. Can you mail a note?

6. Can a pie tell a lie?

1 📖 Read the words in the box.
2 ✏️ Use words from the box and your own words
to write silly questions of your own.

can	you	peach	eat	be	is	Mike	seal	dive	take
have	he	jeep	ride	make	does	it	nose	tune	play
a	she	road	nail	help	did	like	goat	glue	stop

1. Can a seal

2.

3.

ā   ē   ī   ō   ū

Directions: Say each picture name. Listen to the vowel sound. Fill in the space by the word for the picture name.

Example

- ○ rode
- ○ rain
- ○ ram

1. ○ mole ○ mule ○ meal	**2.** ○ pole ○ pile ○ pail	**3.** ○ tide ○ toad ○ tube	**4.** ○ ham ○ hay ○ hid
5. ○ feet ○ fate ○ fail	**6.** ○ cave ○ cone ○ cube	**7.** ○ bat ○ bay ○ bake	**8.** ○ toe ○ tie ○ tile
9. ○ tail ○ tile ○ told	**10.** ○ loaf ○ leaf ○ life	**11.** ○ cone ○ cave ○ coat	**12.** ○ bike ○ bake ○ beak
13. ○ ripe ○ rode ○ robe	**14.** ○ tire ○ tail ○ time	**15.** ○ ram ○ rail ○ ray	**16.** ○ wed ○ weed ○ wide
17. ○ cone ○ cane ○ cute	**18.** ○ bite ○ bait ○ boat	**19.** ○ pole ○ pail ○ peel	**20.** ○ cute ○ cue ○ cut

Testing long vowel sounds; using an adapted standardized test format

Reviewing Long and Short Vowels

a e i o u
ā ē ī ō ū

1 🎵 Say each word.   2 👂 Listen to the vowel sound.
3 ✏️ Circle **S** if you hear a short vowel sound.
Circle **L** if you hear a long vowel sound.
4 ✏️ Print the letter that stands for the vowel sound you hear.

1.	not	Ⓢ	L		11.	tie	S L	
2.	fine	S	L		12.	tree	S L	
3.	cub	S	L		13.	note	S L	
4.	home	S	L		14.	gate	S L	
5.	rain	S	L		15.	pet	S L	
6.	bat	S	L		16.	fun	S L	
7.	lip	S	L		17.	toe	S L	
8.	seat	S	L		18.	line	S L	
9.	spot	S	L		19.	tune	S L	
10.	cube	S	L		20.	ray	S L	

88

Reviewing Long and Short Vowels

1 📖 Read the sentence parts in boxes A, B, and C.

2 ✏️ Make up sentences using the sentence parts and print them on the lines.

Box A	Box B	Box C
Mike and Lee	will swim	to our boat.
The wet seal	ran	by that tree.
An old mule	can stop	at the lake.
Jane and Pam	had lots of fun	on the dunes.
A white hen	rode	on the train.

Mike and Lee rode on the train.

Reviewing Long and Short Vowels

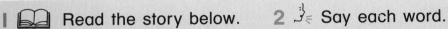

1 📖 Read the story below. 2 🎵 Say each word.

3 👂 Listen carefully to the vowel sounds.

4 ✏️ Draw a line under each word with a long vowel sound.

Many of us have pets. Pets <u>make</u> <u>fine</u> pals.

Jane has a fat cat. It runs at dogs.
Big dogs will run from that cat!

Luke has six red bugs. He keeps them
in a cup. The bugs leap up in the cup.

Ned has a tame hen.
The hen likes to play Hide-and-Seek.

Kim has a cute pig that sleeps in mud.
It likes to play ball.

Bob has a funny white dog.
His dog has six toes on each of its feet!
Bob's dog can beg for bones.

1 📖 Read each question about the story.

2 ✏️ Fill in the space by the correct answer.

1. What does the fat cat do?
   ○ runs at bugs
   ● runs at dogs
   ○ begs for bones
   ○ keeps bugs

2. Where does Luke keep his bugs?
   ○ in a pen
   ○ on his toes
   ○ in the mud
   ○ in a cup

3. What can the tame hen do?
   ○ play Hide and Seek
   ○ eat meat pies
   ○ sleep in the mud
   ○ play ball

4. Which is the best title for this story?
   ○ "A Pet Dog"
   ○ "Pets Are Pals"
   ○ "The Tale of a Mule"
   ○ "A Fat Cat"

Using language arts; reading a story with long and short vowel sounds; story comprehension

a e i o u ā ē ī ō ū

Directions: Read the word in the box. Listen to the vowel sound. Fill in the space below the word with the same vowel sound as the word in the box.

Example

tail	tan ○	ray ○	tab ○

1. boat	bone ○	hot ○	stop ○	12. toe	top ○	soap ○	tot ○
2. pail	pat ○	pay ○	lap ○	13. ten	net ○	tree ○	tea ○
3. can	rain ○	cane ○	cap ○	14. day	pad ○	date ○	dad ○
4. fuse	fun ○	fuss ○	fume ○	15. cube	use ○	cub ○	us ○
5. leaf	let ○	feel ○	led ○	16. tie	pit ○	mitt ○	kite ○
6. tub	but ○	tune ○	tube ○	17. feet	tea ○	fed ○	fell ○
7. bee	best ○	be ○	bed ○	18. top	tone ○	toad ○	pot ○
8. fox	hot ○	doe ○	foal ○	19. seal	see ○	sell ○	set ○
9. like	lip ○	lie ○	lid ○	20. hope	hop ○	hot ○	hoe ○
10. pin	pie ○	pine ○	nip ○	21. sun	up ○	fuse ○	cube ○
11. made	mail ○	add ○	mad ○	22. pan	pane ○	nap ○	pail ○

Hard and Soft c

The letter **c** can stand for two different sounds.
The hard sound of **c** is the sound of **k** as in **kite**.
The soft sound of **c** is the sound of **s** as in **sun**.

cat **c = k**

cent **c = s**

mice **c = s**

1 🗣 Say each picture name.	**2** 👂 Listen to the sound of **c**.	
3 ✏️ Circle the letter that stands for the sound you hear.		

92

Hard and Soft c

The letter **c** followed by **e**, **i**, or **y** usually has the sound of **s** as in **sun**.

ice   pencil

The letter **c** followed by any other letter usually has the sound of **k** as in **kite**.

1 📖 Read each word.
2 👀 Look at the letter that comes after **c**.   3 👆 Say the word.
4 ✏️ Print the word under the sound of **c** you hear.

cub	rice	crib	lace	cape	cent	cup
city	clay	mice	cut	race	cod	place

Hard c (c = k)   **Soft c (c = s)**

cub   rice

Hard and Soft g

The letter **g** can stand for two different sounds.
The hard sound of **g** is the sound of **g** as in **goat**.
The soft sound of **g** is the sound of **j** as in **jet**.

 gate **g**=**g**   cage **g**=**j**   giraffe **g**=**j**

1 🗣 Say each picture name.   2 👂 Listen to the sound of **g**.
3 ✏ Circle the letter that stands for the sound you hear.

(g) j	g j	g j	g j	g j
g j	g j	g j	g j	g j
g j	g j	g j	g j	g j
g j	g j	g j	g j	g j

94

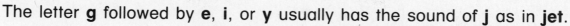

Hard and Soft **g**

The letter **g** followed by **e**, **i**, or **y** usually has the sound of **j** as in **jet**.

cage   giant

The letter **g** followed by any other letter usually has the sound of **g** as in **goat**.

1 Read each word.
2 Look at the letter that comes after **g**.   3 Say the word.
4 Print the word under the sound of **g** you hear.

gate	gym	age	good	gull	gem	stage
cage	got	gave	huge	giant	goat	grass

Hard **g** (**g** = **g**)   Soft **g** (**g** = **j**)

gate   gym

Reviewing Hard and Soft c and g

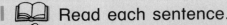

1 📖 Read each sentence.
2 ✏️ Circle the sound of **c** or **g** that you hear in the underlined word.

c

	Hard **c** (**c** = **k**)	Soft **c** (**c** = **s**)
1. The <u>mice</u> will hide from the cat.	k	(s)
2. Carl has a <u>cage</u> for his mice.	k	s
3. Her dress has <u>lace</u> on it.	k	s
4. We had fish and <u>rice</u> to eat.	k	s
5. There is ice in your <u>cup</u>.	k	s
6. Dave needs ten <u>cents</u>.	k	s

g

	Hard **g** (**g** = **g**)	Soft **g** (**g** = **j**)
7. There are many <u>gulls</u> at the sea.	g	j
8. That goat is <u>huge</u>!	g	j
9. We fixed the game with <u>glue</u>.	g	j
10. Gene can read this <u>page</u> to me.	g	j
11. Will we play a game in the <u>gym</u>?	g	j
12. That <u>frog</u> ate the bug.	g	j

Reviewing the hard and soft sounds of **c** and **g**; reading sentences

Hard and Soft **c** and **g**

Directions: Read each word. Fill in the space by the letter that shows which sound the underlined letter stands for.

Example

<u>c</u>ap	○ k ○ s

1. <u>g</u>ate	○ g ○ j	2. <u>c</u>age	○ k ○ s	3. <u>g</u>oat	○ g ○ j	4. <u>c</u>ame	○ k ○ s
5. <u>g</u>ull	○ g ○ j	6. fa<u>c</u>e	○ k ○ s	7. <u>c</u>ute	○ k ○ s	8. pa<u>g</u>e	○ g ○ j
9. <u>c</u>one	○ k ○ s	10. <u>g</u>oes	○ g ○ j	11. ra<u>c</u>e	○ k ○ s	12. hu<u>g</u>e	○ g ○ j
13. <u>c</u>ent	○ k ○ s	14. <u>g</u>em	○ g ○ j	15. i<u>c</u>e	○ k ○ s	16. <u>g</u>ym	○ g ○ j
17. <u>c</u>ity	○ k ○ s	18. a<u>g</u>e	○ g ○ j	19. lo<u>g</u>	○ g ○ j	20. la<u>c</u>e	○ k ○ s

Testing the hard and soft sounds of **c** and **g**; using an adapted standardized test format

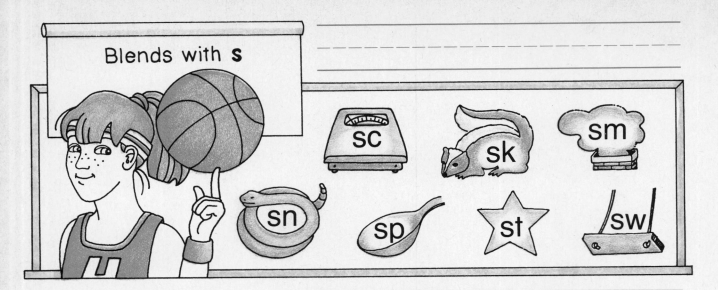

Blends with **s**

sc   sk   sm

sn   sp   st   sw

1 🗣 Say each picture name.   2 👂 Listen to the blend at the beginning.
3 ✏ Circle and then print the letters for the blend you hear.

sk (sp) st	sk sm sw	sn sp st	sc sm sw	sm sn st	sp st sw
_sp_	____	____	____	____	____
sc sm sp	sk sm sn	sp st sw	sm sn sw	sc sp st	sc sm sp
____	____	____	____	____	____
sp st sw	sm sn sp	sc sp st	sk sp st	sc sp sw	sm st sw
____	____	____	____	____	____

Introducing consonant blends with **s**

1 📖 Read the sentence.
2 ✏️ Circle the blend that completes the word in each sentence.
3 ✏️ Print the letters on the line.

1. Dad went up the __st__ eps.

sp	sk	(st)

2. I like to _____ im in the lake.

sk	sw	sn

3. He _____ ips down the street.

sn	sp	sk

4. Mother _____ oke to Miss Jones.

st	sn	sp

5. Step on the _____ ale.

sp	sc	st

6. Can you _____ ell the smoke?

st	sm	sw

7. Does she know how to _____ ate?

sk	st	sp

8. She has a pet _____ ake.

sn	sw	st

9. My coat has a _____ ap.

sp	sw	sn

10. That car did not _____ op!

st	sk	sp

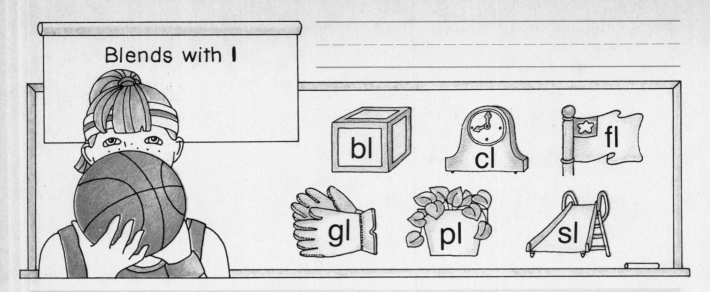

Blends with l

bl   cl   fl
gl   pl   sl

1 🗣 Say each picture name.   2 👂 Listen to the blend at the beginning.
3 ✏ Circle and then print the letters for the blend you hear.

bl **cl** gl
_____
c l

cl gl pl
_____
_____

bl cl fl
_____
_____

fl gl sl
_____
_____

gl pl sl
_____
_____

bl pl sl
_____
_____

bl cl gl
_____
_____

cl fl sl
_____
_____

cl fl pl
_____
_____

bl fl pl
_____
_____

gl pl sl
_____
_____

bl cl pl
_____
_____

gl pl sl
_____
_____

fl pl sl
_____
_____

cl gl pl
_____
_____

bl gl sl
_____
_____

bl cl pl
_____
_____

fl gl sl
_____
_____

Introducing consonant blends with l

1 📖 Read the sentence.
2 ✏️ Circle the blend that completes the word in each sentence.
3 ✏️ Print the letters on the line.

1. You may use my ___gl___ue.

cl (gl) bl

2. Please _____ose the box.

sl   fl   cl

3. Mother gave me a _____ue kite.

bl   fl   gl

4. Did you _____eep on that bed?

cl   sl   bl

5. We can _____ay in his yard.

pl   gl   cl

6. Please keep away from the _____ame.

sl   fl   bl

7. Did you dig for _____ams?

pl   gl   cl

8. I am _____ad you got the pup.

cl   sl   gl

9. The bike has a _____at tire.

gl   cl   fl

10. She will go down the _____ide.

bl   sl   cl

Blends with **r**

1 🗣️ Say each picture name. 2 👂 Listen to the blend at the beginning.
3 ✏️ Circle and then print the letters for the blend you hear.

br (cr) gr	dr pr tr	br pr tr	fr pr tr	cr dr tr	cr fr gr
cr					
gr pr tr	dr gr tr	br fr pr	br dr tr	br cr gr	cr gr pr
fr pr tr	fr gr tr	fr gr tr	br dr gr	fr pr tr	br dr tr

Introducing consonant blends with **r**

Blends with r

1 📖 Read the sentence.
2 ✏️ Circle the blend that completes the word in each sentence.
3 ✏️ Print the letters on the line.

1. She can ___ dr ___ive that truck. | br   tr   (dr) |

2. I got a _____ize for the best story. | pr   cr   gr |

3. The _____ab was in the pail. | br   fr   cr |

4. I _____oke the plate. | dr   br   pr |

5. We will run to that _____ee. | fr   br   tr |

6. A _____og lives by the lake. | tr   fr   gr |

7. The grass is _____een. | gr   cr   pr |

8. We got a _____ee ride. | fr   gr   dr |

9. I have a _____ay cat. | br   gr   cr |

10. The _____ain was very late. | tr   cr   gr |

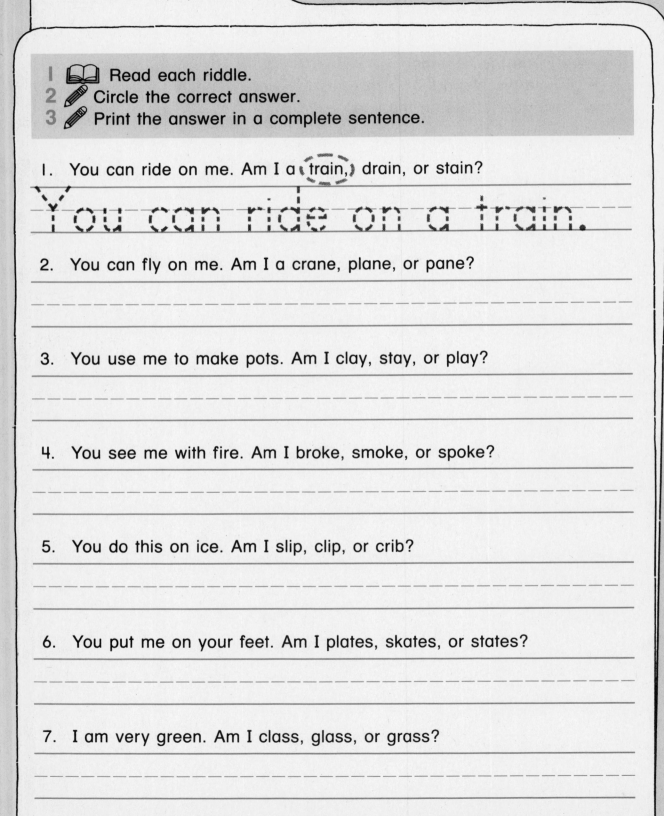

Reviewing Blends with **s**, **l**, **r**

1 📖 Read each riddle.
2 ✏️ Circle the correct answer.
3 ✏️ Print the answer in a complete sentence.

1. You can ride on me. Am I a (train,) drain, or stain?

You can ride on a train.

2. You can fly on me. Am I a crane, plane, or pane?

3. You use me to make pots. Am I clay, stay, or play?

4. You see me with fire. Am I broke, smoke, or spoke?

5. You do this on ice. Am I slip, clip, or crib?

6. You put me on your feet. Am I plates, skates, or states?

7. I am very green. Am I class, glass, or grass?

Reviewing consonant blends with **s**, **l**, and **r**; writing sentences

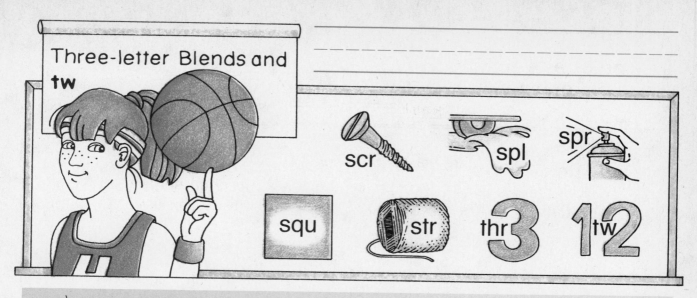

Three-letter Blends and tw

scr

spl

spr

squ

str

thr 3

1 tw 2

1 ☼ Say each picture name. 2 👂 Listen to the blend at the beginning.
3 ✏ Circle and then print the letters for the blend you hear.

spl squ (str)	scr spl spr	spl squ spr	str thr tw	scr str thr	scr spr squ
str					

spl spr str	squ thr tw	scr spr thr	str thr tw	scr spl spr	scr squ tw

str thr tw	spl spr thr	spl spr str	scr thr tw	scr spl squ	scr squ tw

Introducing consonant blends with three letters and **tw**

1 📖 Read the sentence.
2 ✏️ Circle the blend that completes the word in each sentence.
3 ✏️ Print the letters on the line.

1. Do you live on this 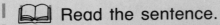 ____str____eet?

   scr (str) squ

2. Give the tube a _____eeze.

   squ   scr   str

3. Jane has _____ee cats.

   spr   thr   spl

4. We sat so we could see the _____een.

   scr   str   squ

5. We _____ay the grass to keep it green.

   spl   squ   spr

6. I have a _____in who looks like me.

   sc   sm   tw

7. _____ub the tub to get it clean.

   Spr   Scr   Str

8. Did you hear the pig _____eal?

   scr   str   squ

9. I like to _____ash in the lake.

   scr   spr   spl

10. The bug sat on a _____ig.

    tw   sm   st

106

Final Blends

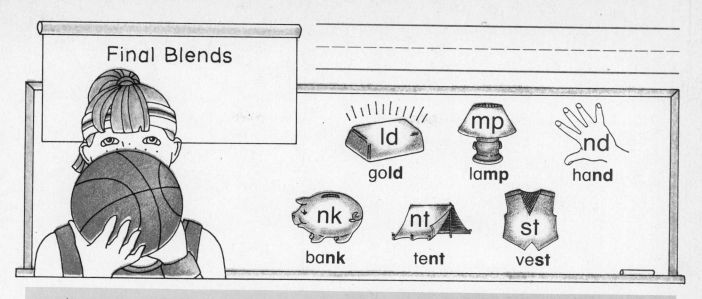

gold   lamp   hand

bank   tent   vest

1 Say each picture name.   **2** Listen to the blend at the end.
3 Circle and then print the letters for the blend you hear.

nd nk nt	nd nk nt	ld nt st	mp nd nt	ld mp nt	mp nk st
n d					
nk nt st	mp nd nt	nd nt st	ld nk st	ld nd nt	nd nk nt
nd nk nt	mp nt st	ld mp nk	nd nk nt	nd nk nt	ld mp st

1 📖 Read the sentence.
2 ✏️ Circle the blend that completes the word in each sentence.
3 ✏️ Print the letters on the line.

1. We will ca __mp__ at the lake.

| nk | (mp) | nd |

2. This dress is very o_____.

| ld | nd | st |

3. I hit the ball with my ha_____.

| st | nd | nt |

4. She had to hu_____ for her skates.

| ld | nt | st |

5. They can run fa_____.

| nk | mp | st |

6. Please put the plate in the si_____.

| nd | nt | nk |

7. There is a la_____ in the tent.

| nt | mp | ld |

8. I thi_____ I have your book.

| nd | st | nk |

9. I we_____ to play with Dad.

| nt | mp | nk |

10. The bank put the go_____ in the safe.

| nd | mp | ld |

Using language arts; using sentence context to complete words with blends in final position

Reviewing Final Blends, 3-letter Blends, and **tw**

1 📖 Read each riddle.
2 ✏️ Circle the correct answer.
3 ✏️ Print the answer in a complete sentence.

1. I am on a kite. Am I a thing, spring, or (string)?

A string is on a kite.

2. I can be on a tree. Am I a wig, pig, or twig?

3. I can hold eggs. Am I a nest, best, or test?

4. You use me to clap. Am I a stand, hand, or band?

5. I have four sides. Am I a spare, stare, or square?

6. I come after two. Am I three, tree, or free?

7. You can do this when you sleep. Am I stream, steam, or dream?

Unit Review: blends

sm oke	ag	si	int
pla	ee	fo	ess
ig	ash	one ne	
ed	la	een	ame
own	ing	ha	ill

110

Unit Review: blends

1. Can a fly spy a plum?
   _____

   yes

2. Can a clock fold its hands?
   _____

3. Can a fast plane streak across
   the sky? _____

4. Will three snails have twelve
   trails? _____
   _____

5. Can a tree grow in a sink?
   _____

6. Is a squeal the same as a
   squeak? _____

1 📖 Read the words in the box.
2 ✏️ Use words from the box and your own words
to write silly questions of your own.

can	it	sled	stand	twins	is	that	plate	grass	throne
will	you	clam	drum	street	did	jump	flute	ask	squeal
have	she	skate	truck	throw	the	does	slip	grab	last

1. Can a clam _____

2. _____

3. _____

Blends

Directions: Fill in the space next to the blend that will complete the word.

Example

- ○ ld
- ○ st
- ○ nt

la___

1. ○ sk ○ bl ○ dr ___ate	2. ○ fr ○ cl ○ sn ___ake	3. ○ gl ○ sp ○ pr ___ot	4. ○ nt ○ ng ○ mp la___
5. ○ fr ○ sw ○ pl ___im	6. ○ bl ○ sp ○ sn ___ue	7. ○ tr ○ st ○ cl ___ose	8. ○ cr ○ fl ○ gr ___ute
9. ○ dr ○ st ○ gl ___ad	10. ○ nt ○ st ○ nd ba___	11. ○ gr ○ sk ○ sl ___eep	12. ○ br ○ sp ○ fl ___ave
13. ○ cr ○ gl ○ sm ___ab	14. ○ sk ○ cl ○ dr ___ive	15. ○ tw ○ sc ○ sm ___are	16. ○ sn ○ sc ○ sm ___oke
17. ○ spl ○ scr ○ spr ___eam	18. ○ spl ○ str ○ scr ___ash	19. ○ squ ○ thr ○ spr ___ing	20. ○ str ○ scr ○ squ ___eet

Testing consonant blends; using an adapted standardized test format

Sounds of **y**

y = y   y = ē   y = ī

1 🗣 Say each picture name.   2 👂 Listen to the sound of **y**.
3 ✏️ Circle the letter that stands for the sound of **y** you hear.

fly	ē ⓘ y	baby	ē ī y	yarn	ē ī y	spy	ē ī y
penny	ē ī y	yo-yo	ē ī y	cry	ē ī y	yawn	ē ī y
year	ē ī y	sky	ē ī y	bunny	ē ī y	yell	ē ī y
try	ē ī y	happy	ē ī y	yard	ē ī y	pony	ē ī y
puppy	ē ī y	dry	ē ī y	yam	ē ī y	twenty	ē ī y

Sounds of **y**

1 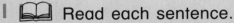 Read each sentence.
2 ✏ Circle each word with the letter **y**.   3 Ᵹ Say the word.
4 ✏ Print the word in the column for the sound of **y** you hear.

1. (Why) did (you) (cry)?

2. Daddy will read a story to the baby.

3. It is sunny and the sky is blue.

4. Have you ever seen a yak?

5. Did you try to ride the pony yet?

6. This big coat will keep me dry.

y = ē	**y = ī**	**y = y**
	Why	you
	cry	

Using language arts; using sentence context to identify words with the sounds of **y**: /ē/, /ī/, /y/

1 📖 Read each sentence.   2 ✏️ Circle the word
with the same sound of **y** as the underlined word.
3 ✏️ Print the word on the line to complete the sentence.

1. Do you think <u>my</u> coat is dry ?

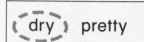

(dry) pretty

2. We are <u>happy</u> with our new _____ .

puppy   sky

3. I need some <u>yellow</u> _____ .

cry   yarn

4. A _____ is not <u>very</u> much.

year   penny

5. The <u>baby</u> is very _____ .

happy   yours

6. <u>Why</u> are you looking at the _____ ?

pony   sky

7. Can a <u>yak</u> eat a _____ ?

yam   fly

8. I can _____ the <u>bunny</u>.

carry   dry

9. We liked the <u>funny</u> _____ .

fly   story

10. I will <u>try</u> not to _____ .

hurry   cry

Sounds of **y**

Directions: Read the word in the box. Listen to the sound of **y**. Fill in the space below the word that does **not** have the same sound of **y**.

Example

pony	why ○	baby ○	happy ○

1. lady	story ○	fly ○	happy ○	12. dry	penny ○	why ○	sky ○
2. cry	fry ○	funny ○	fly ○	13. my	bunny ○	fly ○	try ○
3. city	sky ○	happy ○	pony ○	14. sunny	happy ○	by ○	many ○
4. silly	why ○	very ○	bunny ○	15. by	try ○	very ○	shy ○
5. story	penny ○	my ○	sunny ○	16. happy	bunny ○	daddy ○	yes ○
6. by	any ○	shy ○	fly ○	17. try	fly ○	pretty ○	sky ○
7. daddy	sunny ○	why ○	happy ○	18. dry	many ○	my ○	shy ○
8. sky	cry ○	try ○	hurry ○	19. yam	yell ○	pony ○	yet ○
9. many	try ○	puppy ○	daddy ○	20. my	funny ○	fly ○	cry ○
10. sunny	pretty ○	happy ○	fly ○	21. city	very ○	cry ○	puppy ○
11. yet	yak ○	carry ○	yell ○	22. story	yes ○	carry ○	happy ○

116

Digraphs:
ch, sh, th, wh

1 ☝ Say each picture name.   2 👂 Listen to the first sound.
3 ✏ Print the letters that stand for the sound you hear
at the beginning of each picture name.

1 📖 Read each sentence.
2 ✏️ Circle the letters that complete the word in each sentence.
3 ✏️ Print the letters on the line.

1. Fran has a bike with two __wh__ eels.

ch sh th (wh)

2. Stan likes _____ ese fine ties.

ch sh th wh

3. If you do not eat, you will get too _____ in.

ch sh th wh

4. Mom will _____ op up some logs for the fire.

ch sh th wh

5. My dad _____ aves his face each day.

ch sh th wh

6. Pam likes to eat _____ eese on a bun.

ch sh th wh

7. The tail of a _____ ale is huge!

ch sh th wh

8. We sailed on the ocean in a big _____ ip.

ch sh th wh

9. The baby has fat rosy _____ eeks.

ch sh th wh

10. Wave to them _____ en they leave.

ch sh th wh

Using language arts; using sentence context to complete words with initial consonant digraphs:
ch, sh, th, wh

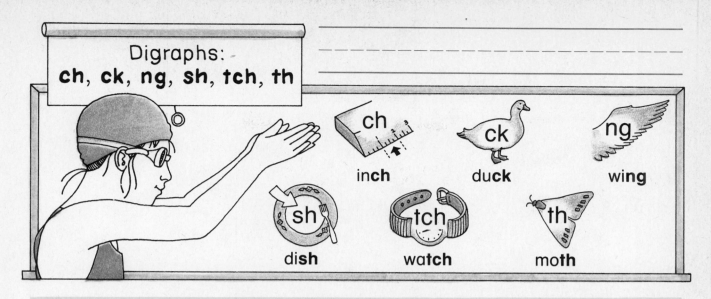

Digraphs:
ch, **ck**, **ng**, **sh**, **tch**, **th**

in**ch** du**ck** wi**ng**

di**sh** wa**tch** mo**th**

1 ✌ Say each picture name. 2 👂 Listen to the last sound.
3 ✏ Circle and then print the letters that stand for the sound
you hear at the end of each picture name.

ch (sh) ck	ch sh th	ck tch ng	ch sh ck	ch ck ng	tch sh th
sh					
ch sh th	tch th ck	sh th tch	ch th ng	tch sh ck	ch sh th
tch ck ng	ch sh th	ch sh ng	tch th ck	tch sh th	ch sh ck

_____

_____

1 📖 Read each sentence.
2 ✏ Circle the letters that complete the word in each sentence.
3 ✏ Print the letters on the line.

1. Jean likes to play on the swi __ng__ .

ch th ck (ng)

2. That fi _____ has a huge fin.

tch sh th ng

3. Chuck lit the fire with a ma _____ .

tch sh th ck

4. What a pretty gold ri _____ !

sh th ck ng

5. May I have a bite of that pea _____ ?

ch sh th ck

6. That muddy dog needs a ba _____ .

ch sh th ng

7. Please ta _____ that page on the wall.

ch sh ck ng

8. Brad drove the big blue tru _____ .

ch sh ck ng

9. Can you rea _____ that glass of milk?

ch sh th ng

10. Dad needs to pa _____ that hole.

tch sh th ck

Using language arts; using sentence context to complete words with final consonant digraphs:
ch, ck, ng, sh, tch, th

Reviewing Digraphs

1 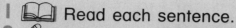 Read each sentence.
2 ✏ Circle the words that make sense in the sentence.

1. Please (check) / catch your wash / (watch) for the time.

2. Which thin / thing do you wish / witch for the most?

3. How many cheese / shells are on this back / beach ?

4. Brick / Bring two pairs of socks / songs on the trip.

5. Mom needs to catch / cash a shack / check at the store.

6. After luck / lunch , we will sick / sing some songs.

7. The hen likes to chase / shake her chick / thick around the yard.

8. Which path / patch goes to the berry patch / path ?

9. The dog will wash / watch over the sheep / cheep .

10. Can a wait / whale be white / which ?

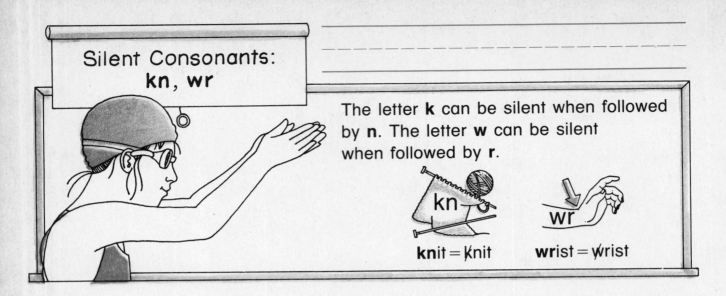

Silent Consonants: kn, wr

The letter **k** can be silent when followed by **n**. The letter **w** can be silent when followed by **r**.

knit = ḵnit   **wr**ist = ẉrist

---

1 Say each picture name.   2 Listen to the first sound.
3 Print the letters that stand for the sound you hear at the beginning of each picture name.

wr	____	____	____	____
____	____	____	____	____
____	____	____	____	____
____	____	____	____	____

Introducing silent consonants: **kn**, **wr**

1 📖 Read each sentence.
2 ✏️ Circle the letters that complete the word in each sentence.
3 ✏️ Print the letters on the line.

1. The __kn__ ife has a dull blade.

(kn)   wr

2. Did Brad _____ ock at the door?

kn   wr

3. Beth will _____ ite a note to Dad.

kn   wr

4. Fran had a scrape on her _____ ee.

kn   wr

5. Mom needs a _____ ench to fix the bike.

kn   wr

6. Tim had a cast on his _____ ist.

kn   wr

7. Blake knows how to _____ it.

kn   wr

8. Chet made a _____ ot in his tie.

kn   wr

9. Did you see that _____ en in the tree?

kn   wr

10. Please ask Karl to _____ ap my gift.

kn   wr

Reviewing Silent Consonants: kn, wr

1 📖 Read each sentence.
2 ✏️ Circle the words that make sense in the sentence.

1. Use a ~~wren~~
    (wrench) to fix the (wheel) .
                        shell

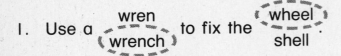

2. Kim needs a knife to cut her reach .
                 knock   peach

3. We made a wreck   from a pine branch .
               wreath   bench

4. Please knock the sand off the check .
            knot   shell

5. Watch her wrong out the wet rag.
    Catch   wring

6. Can you tie a knot in that long rope?
                   knob   song

7. The wrench broke its ring and will not fly.
         wren   wing

8. Keep your wrist stiff when you hit the ball back .
              write   sack

9. Meg likes to knit with white string .
                  knot   strong

10. Sam fell on the path and cut his knee .
                     pat   kneel

1 📖 Read each sentence.
2 ✏️ Circle the letters that complete the word in each sentence.
3 ✏️ Print the letters on the line.

1. Can you pu __sh__ me in the swing?

th sh wh tch

2. Brush your tee_____ before you go to bed.

wh ch th ck

3. The _____eel came off my bike.

wr wh sh ch

4. Do you see the _____en in the tree?

kn wr th wh

5. We ate lun_____ at the beach.

ck ch th ng

6. Dave gave Pam a ri_____.

th ck ng ch

7. Tim likes to play with his tru_____.

ch sh ck ng

8. When you kneel, you sit on your _____ees.

ch th kn sh

9. Dad needs a ma_____ to make a fire.

th ck ch tch

10. Can you hear the _____imes ring?

ch sh wh wr

1 📖 Read each riddle.
2 ✏️ Circle the correct answer.
3 ✏️ Print the answer in a complete sentence.

1. I can lock a box. Am I a train, (chain) or crane?

A chain can lock a box.

2. I can make a fire. Am I a match, hatch, or patch?

3. You can make me with string. Am I a knot, trot, or shot?

4. You need a brain to do this. Am I drink, think, or shrink?

5. I can make a splash. Am I a trail, stale, or whale?

6. I help planes fly. Am I wings, sings, or wrings?

7. You will yell if you step on me. Am I a tack, pack, or sack?

Unit review: using riddles to identify words and write sentences with words
with consonant digraphs or silent consonants

Digraphs and Silent Consonants

Directions: Fill in the space next to the letters that will complete the word.

Example

- ○ ch
- ○ sh
- ○ th

___ill

1. ○ ck ○ ch ○ th ___ain	2. ○ th ○ tch ○ sh bru___	3. ○ wh ○ kn ○ th ___in	4. ○ ng ○ wh ○ ck tri___
5. ○ wh ○ ch ○ kn ___ot	6. ○ th ○ sh ○ wh pa___	7. ○ wh ○ ch ○ ck lun___	8. ○ wr ○ wh ○ sh ___ap
9. ○ tch ○ wr ○ sh pi___	10. ○ wh ○ sh ○ kn ___en	11. ○ ck ○ kn ○ th ___ock	12. ○ tch ○ wh ○ th ___ank
13. ○ ch ○ sh ○ wr ___ite	14. ○ wh ○ ch ○ th ___ase	15. ○ sh ○ ck ○ ch ne___	16. ○ sh ○ th ○ ch ___ut
17. ○ ng ○ wh ○ tch ma___	18. ○ sh ○ ng ○ th si___	19. ○ sh ○ wr ○ wh wi___	20. ○ ch ○ th ○ wh ___ite

Vowels with r: **ar**

Star has the sound of **ar**.

st**ar** ⭐

1 🗣 Say each picture name.   2 👂 Listen for the sound of **ar**.
3 ✏️ Print **ar** if you hear that sound.
4 ✏️ Then go back and print the letter or letters
for the other sounds of **a** you hear.

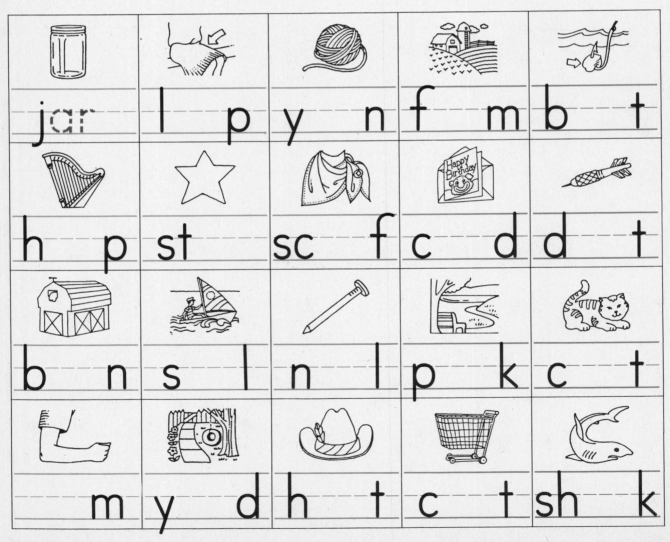

j**ar**	l	p y n	f m b	t
h	p st	sc f c	d d	t
b	n s l	n l p	k c	t
m y	d h	t c	t sh	k

128

1 📖 Read each riddle.
2 ✏️ Circle the correct answer.
3 ✏️ Print the answer in a complete sentence.

1. You can knit with me. Am I yard, year, or (yarn?)

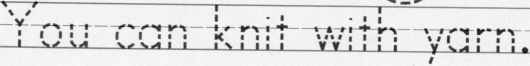

You can knit with yarn.

2. I am on a tree. Am I bark, barn, or harm?

3. You send me to a pal. Am I a part, card, or dark?

4. I am not close. Am I jar, car, or far?

5. You can play in me. Am I a yard, hard, or yarn?

6. Horses sleep in me. Am I a park, barn, or harm?

7. I shine in the sky. Am I a sharp, star, or start?

Vowels with r: or

Fork has the sound of **or**.

f**or**k

1 Say each picture name.   2 Listen for the sound of **or**.
3 Print **or** if you hear that sound.
4 Then go back and print the letters for the other
sounds you hear.

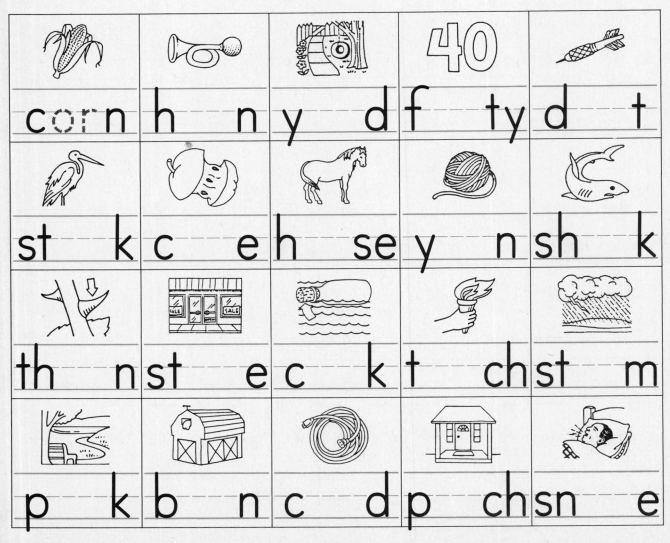

c o r n	h n	y	d f	t y d	t
st k	c	e h	se y	n sh	k
th n	st	e c	k t	ch st	m
p k	b	n c	d p	ch sn	e

Introducing **r**-controlled vowels: **or**

Vowels with r: or

1 📖 Read each riddle.
2 ✏️ Circle the correct answer.
3 ✏️ Print the answer in a complete sentence.

1. I am not long. Am I (short) sort, or sport?

Short is not long.

2. You can get food from me. Am I a score, more, or store?

_____

_____

3. I bring wind and rain. Am I a fort, sort, or storm?

_____

_____

4. I am in an apple. Am I a snore, store, or core?

_____

_____

5. You use me to eat. Am I a pork, fork, or cork?

_____

_____

6. You can pop and eat me. Am I horn, torn, or corn?

_____

_____

7. I can stick in you. Am I a storm, shore, or thorn?

_____

_____

Reviewing **ar** and **or**

1 📖 Read each sentence.

2 ✏️ Print **ar** or **or** to complete both words in each sentence.

1. Where did he p __ar__ k his c __ar__ ?

2. The h _____ se ate all the c _____ n.

3. You can see st _____ s when it is d _____ k.

4. We will write a sh _____ t st _____ y.

5. I saw a b _____ n on the f _____ m.

6. The sharp th _____ ns have t _____ n my sleeve.

7. How f _____ is it to the p _____ k?

8. Put this t _____ ch on the p _____ ch.

9. Our p _____ ty will st _____ t soon.

10. We saw the st _____ m from our p _____ ch.

Vowels with **r**: **er**, **ir**, **ur**

The letters **er**, **ir**, and **ur** make the same sound.

f**er**n   b**ir**d   p**ur**se

1 Say each picture name.   **2** Listen for the sound of **er**, **ir**, or **ur**.
3 Print **er**, **ir**, or **ur** to complete each picture name.
The letters in dark print show which spelling to use in each column.

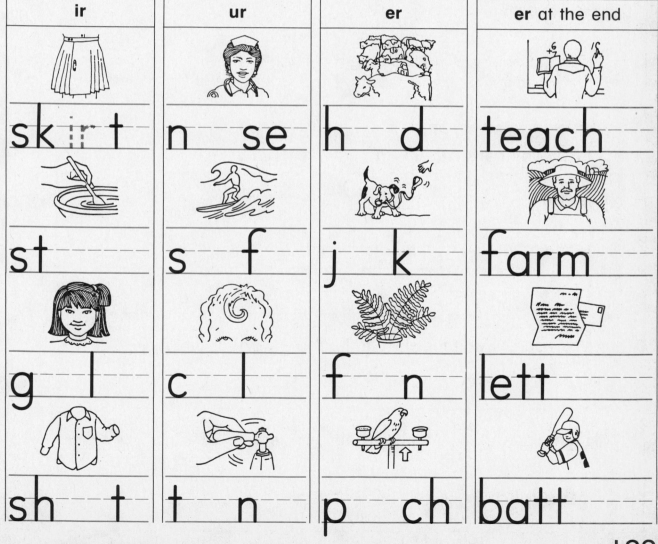

ir	ur	er	er at the end
sk**ir**t	n se	h d	teach
st	s f	j k	farm
g l	c l	f n	lett
sh t	t n	p ch	batt

1. 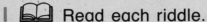 Read each riddle.
2. ✏ Circle the correct answer.
3. ✏ Print the answer in a complete sentence.

1. I can make you sick. Am I a term, (germ) or fern?

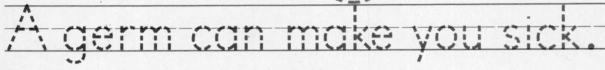
A germ can make you sick.

2. A bird sits on me. Am I a perch, chirp, or shirt?

_____

_____

3. I am not a boy. Am I a curl, girl, or hurl?

_____

_____

4. I help you get well. Am I a purse, nurse, or first?

_____

_____

5. I am not last. Am I firm, first, or hurt?

_____

_____

6. You need to wait for me. Am I a fern, stern, or turn?

_____

_____

7. I am a seal's coat. Am I fur, purr, or her?

_____

_____

1. Read each sentence.
2. Print **ar**, **or**, **er**, **ir**, or **ur** to complete both words in each sentence.

1. Mark went to the st___or___e for m___or___e milk.

2. We rode in Dad's c_____ to the f_____m.

3. Kate put h_____ bird on its p_____ch.

4. Please wait your t_____n to see the n_____se.

5. Get that h_____se off our p_____ch!

6. That g_____l has a fine, red sk_____t.

7. We must leave the p_____k when it is d_____k.

8. F_____st, you have to st_____ the soup.

9. That st_____m has hurt our c_____n.

10. Mitch was too sh_____t to reach that f_____k.

Unit Review: vowels with r

1 📖 Read the sentence.
2 ✏️ Circle the letters that complete the word in each sentence.
3 ✏️ Print the letters on the line.

_____
1. A b 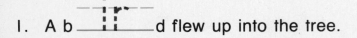 **ir** d flew up into the tree.

| (ir) or ar |

_____
2. Marta got a lett _____ in the mail.

| or ar er |

_____
3. Carlos rode a h _____ se on the farm.

| ur or ar |

_____
4. Let's go to the p _____ k to play.

| er or ar |

_____
5. H _____ ry or you will be late!

| ur ar or |

_____
6. We can plant a f _____ n by that tree.

| or er ar |

_____
7. Mom took her p _____ se with her.

| ar or ur |

_____
8. We ate c _____ n for lunch.

| or ir ar |

_____
9. It is too d _____ k to play in the yard.

| er ar or |

_____
10. Mark is f _____ st in line.

| ir or ar |

1 📖 Read each silly question.
2 ✏️ Print **yes** or **no** to answer the question.

1. Can a farm be in a barn?

no

2. Is a shirt a bird?

3. Can a shark play cards?

4. Can a girl turn into a bird?

5. Can a horse be born in a barn?

6. Does a fern have fur?

1 📖 Read the words in the box.
2 ✏️ Use words from the box and your own words
to write silly questions of your own.

Mark	nurse	farmer	shirt	herd	letter	her	burn	is
horn	shark	corn	park	bird	a	can	did	will	turn
girl	fur	Kurt	the	have	car	skirt	for	get	horse	in

1. Can a shark

2.

3.

1 📖 Read the words in the box. 2 📖 Read each clue.
3 ✏️ Write the correct word in the puzzle.

corn	bird	arm
hers	park	burn
fern	star	girl
horse		hurts

ACROSS

2. This can fly.
4. You can eat this on the cob.
6. This is not a boy.
7. If it is not his, it is _____.
9. This shines in a dark sky.

DOWN

1. This is a green plant.
2. A fire can do this.
3. You can ride on this.
5. This is a place with grass and trees.
7. If you get a cut, it does this.
8. This is a part of you.

Unit review: using words with **r**-controlled vowels to complete a crossword puzzle

1 📖 Read the story below. 2 🎵 Say each word.
3 👂 Listen carefully to the vowel sounds.
4 ✏️ Draw a line under each word with a vowel with **r**.

Last <u>summer</u> I went to stay on <u>Grandfather's</u> farm.
There was a baby horse on the farm.
I saw it just after it was born.
There were many birds, too.
One lark sang to me every morning.
It said, "Chirp, chirp."

There was a herd of goats on the farm.
The goats ate grass under a big fir tree.
They also ate the ferns by the porch.
Then they ate the corn!

I loved my first stay on the farm.
I want to go back next summer.

1 📖 Read each question about the story.
2 ✏️ Fill in the space by the correct answer.

1. What was born on the farm?
   ○ a baby goat
   ○ a lark
   ○ a fern
   ● a baby horse

2. A lark is
   ○ a horse.
   ○ a bird.
   ○ a goat.
   ○ a chirp.

3. The goats ate
   ○ just the ferns by the porch.
   ○ just the grass.
   ○ just the corn.
   ○ the ferns, the grass, and the corn.

4. Which is the best title for this story?
   ○ "Birth of a Horse"
   ○ "A Barn on the Farm"
   ○ "A Summer on a Farm"
   ○ "A Goat by the Porch"

ar er ir or ur

Directions: Say each picture name. Listen to the vowel sound. Fill in the space next to the letters that stand for the sound you hear in the picture name.

Example

○ or
○ ar
○ ur

1. ○ or ○ ar ○ ir	2. ○ er ○ ar ○ or	3. ○ or ○ ir ○ ar	4. ○ ar ○ ur ○ or
5. ○ ar ○ or ○ ur	6. ○ ir ○ or ○ ar	7. ○ ar ○ ur ○ or	8. ○ ir ○ ar ○ or
9. ○ ar ○ ur ○ or	10. ○ or ○ er ○ ar	11. ○ ar ○ or ○ ur	12. ○ er ○ ar ○ or
13. ○ ar ○ ir ○ or	14. ○ or ○ ar ○ ur	15. ○ ar ○ er ○ or	16. ○ ar ○ ur ○ or
17. ○ ar ○ or ○ er	18. ○ or ○ er ○ ar	19. ○ ar ○ ir ○ or	20. ○ or ○ ar ○ ur

140

Testing **r**-controlled vowels; using an adapted standardized test format

Vowel Sounds with oo

The letters **oo** can stand for the sound you hear in **book**.

book

wood

1 🗣 Say each picture name.
2 👂 Listen for the sound of **oo** you hear in **book**.
3 ✏️ Find the word in the box and print it on the line.

book	brook	cook	foot	good	look
stood	shook	crook	wood	hood	hook

shook

___

___

___

___

___

___

___

___

___

___

___

Vowel Sounds with **oo**

The letters **oo** can stand for the sound you hear in **moon**.

moon

spoon

1 🗣 Say each picture name.
2 👂 Listen for the sound of **oo** you hear in **moon**.
3 ✏️ Find the word in the box and print it on the line.

| moose | bloom | boot | food | loose | moo |
| moon | pool | loop | roof | stool | spoon |

roof

Vowel Sounds with **oo**

The letters **oo** can stand for the sound you hear in **book** or the sound you hear in **moon**.

book moon

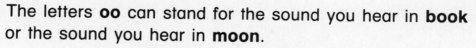

1 📖 Read each word. 2 👂 Listen to the sound of **oo**.
3 ✏️ Find the column with the same sound of **oo** and print the word by its picture.

wood	moose	food	brook	roof	book	stool
hook	pool	stood	shook	moon	boot	hood

oo as in **book**   **oo** as in **moon**

book   moon

Vowel Sounds with **ew**

The letters **ew** can stand for the same sound as the letters **oo** in **moon**.

flew

1. 🗣 Say each picture name.
2. 👂 Listen for the sound of **ew** you hear in **flew**.
3. ✏ Find the word in the box and print it on the line.

blew	chew	drew	Lew	flew	grew
new	threw	dew	screw	crew	stew

flew

1 📖 Read each riddle.
2 ✏️ Choose the answer from the box and print it on the line.

chew	stool	moon	new	grew
brook	spoon	foot	pool	

1. This is in the sky. moon

2. You do this with your teeth. _____

3. You can eat with this. _____

4. You can put a sock on me. _____

5. You did this when you got bigger. _____

6. You can swim in me. _____

7. You can sit on this. _____

8. I am a little stream. _____

9. I am not old. _____

Vowel Sounds with **au**, **aw**

The letters **au** and **aw** can stand for the same sound.

auto

saw

1 🗣 Say each picture name.
2 👂 Listen for the sound of **au** and **aw** you hear in **auto** and **saw**.
3 ✏️ Find the word in the box and print it on the line.

| fawn | lawn | yawn | sauce | hawk | auto |
| claws | haul | paw | gauze | jaw | draw |

jaw

Vowel Sounds with **au**, **aw**

1 📖 Read each riddle.
2 ✏️ Choose the answer from the box and print it on the line.

hawk jaw dawn pause yawn
lawn auto straw raw

1. You do this when you need sleep.

2. I have green grass.   _____

3. I am a bird.   _____

4. You can ride down the road in me.   _____

5. You can sip drinks with this.   _____

6. I am when the sun comes up.   _____

7. I am not cooked.   _____

8. I am not a full stop.   _____

9. I go up and down when you chew.   _____

Vowel Sounds with **ea**

The letters **ea** can stand for the sound you hear in **bread**.

bread

1. 🗣 Say each picture name.
2. 👂 Listen for the sound of **ea** you hear in **bread**.
3. ✏️ Find the word in the box and print it on the line.

lead	leather	thread	head	bread	sweater
ready	read	breath	feather	heavy	weather

breath

Vowel Sounds with **ea**

1 📖 Read each riddle.
2 ✏️ Choose the answer from the box and print it on the line.

bread	feathers	head	weather	thread
heavy	ready	sweater	breath	

1. You can knit this from wool.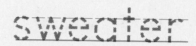

2. A duck has a lot of these. _____

3. You can find this on top of a neck. _____

4. You can toast this. _____

5. A rip can be fixed with this. _____

6. This is good when the sun shines. _____

7. You must be this before you begin. _____

8. Take a deep one of these. _____

9. This is not light. _____

Reviewing Vowel Sounds with **au**, **aw**, **ea**, **ew**, **oo**

1 Read each silly question.
2 Print **yes** or **no** to answer the question.

1. Can a cook look good?

    yes

2. Can a moose be on the loose?

3. Will a screw taste good in stew?

4. Can a thread take a breath?

5. Can a claw be on a paw?

6. Can a fawn drive an auto?

---

1 Read the words in the box.
2 Use words from the box and your own words to write silly questions of your own.

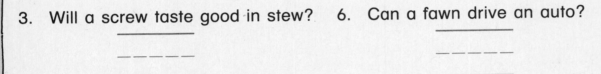

cook	good	brook	shook	be	is	to	goose	moon	bloom
haul	yawn	fawn	sauce	auto	in	stew	chew	screw	new
can	with	an	bread	thread	head	feather	on	the	get

1. _Can a goose_

2.

3.

Reviewing vowel digraphs; reading and writing sentences with words with digraphs

Vowel Sounds with **ow**

The letters **ow** can stand for the sound you hear in **cow**.

cow

1. 🗣 Say each picture name.
2. 👂 Listen for the sound of **ow** you hear in **cow**.
3. ✏️ Find the word in the box and print it on the line.

| plow | owl | clown | tower | flower | bow |
| cow | town | howl | down | crown | gown |

flower

Vowel Sounds with **ow**

The letters **ow** can stand for the long sound of **o**.

snow

crow

1. ☞ Say each picture name.
2. 👂 Listen for the long sound of **o** you hear in **snow** and **crow**.
3. ✏ Find the word in the box and print it on the line.

| bow | bowl | blow | row | grow | mow |
| glow | snow | crow | tow | low | throw |

grow

Vowel Sounds with **ow**

The letters **ow** can stand for the sound you hear in **cow** or the sound you hear in **snow**.

cow   snow

owl	row	mow	flower	clown	crow	low
down	throw	tower	town	slow	grow	plow

ow as in **cow**   **ow** as in **snow**

owl   low

Vowel Sounds with **ou**

The letters **ou** can stand for the same sound as the letters **ow** in **cow**.

mouse

1. 🗣 Say each picture name.
2. 👂 Listen for the sound of **ou** you hear in **mouse**.
3. ✏️ Find the word in the box and print it on the line.

mouth	blouse	house	cloud	ground	bounce
round	couch	mound	pouch	hound	mouse

round

1 📖 Read each riddle.
2 ✏️ Choose the answer from the box and print it on the line.

shout	owl	snow	throw	house
ground	cloud	town	slow	

1. I ask, "Who? Who? Who?" owl

2. This is cold and white. _____

3. I am in the sky. _____

4. You can do this to a ball. _____

5. You can dig in me. _____

6. I am not fast. _____

7. I am very loud. _____

8. You can live in one of these. _____

9. I am a little city. _____

Using language arts; using context clues to identify and print vowel digraphs and diphthongs:
ow as /ō/, **ow**, **ou** as /ou/

155

Vowel Sounds with **oi, oy**

The letters **oi** and **oy** can stand for the same sound.

coin

boy

1 Say each picture name.
2 Listen for the sound of **oi** and **oy** you hear in **coin** and **boy**.
3 Find the word in the box and print it on the line.

| coin | boil | boy | soil | oil | point |
| toy | voice | joy | noise | foil | choice |

boil

1. 📖 Read each riddle.
2. ✏️ Choose the answer from the box and print it on the line.

choice	toy	noise	soil	voice
boy	point	joy	coin	

1. I am any sound.   noise

2. You can play with me.   _____

3. You use me to talk.   _____

4. I will grow up to be a man.   _____

5. A dime is one of them.   _____

6. I am filled with happiness!   _____

7. I am what you pick.   _____

8. You can plant seeds in me.   _____

9. I am sharp.   _____

1 📖 Read each silly question.
2 ✏️ Print **yes** or **no** to answer the question.

1. Will a crow grow a crown?

    no

2. Can a crowd shout, "Ouch!"?

3. Does a brown cow have a voice?

4. Can a boy with a bow take a bow?

5. Will a flower point to a clown?

6. Can a toy make a noise?

1 📖 Read the words in the box.
2 ✏️ Use words from the box and your own words
to write silly questions of your own.

clown	grow	an	crown	shout	ouch	owl	the	bow	now
gown	toy	flower	show	mouth	will	can	voice	point	a
to	with	clouds	coin	loud	brown	is	ground	boy	crow

1. Can a toy

2.

3.

Reviewing vowel digraphs and diphthongs; reading and writing sentences with words with digraphs and diphthongs

Unit Review: other vowel sounds

1 📖 Read each sentence.
2 ✏ Circle the letters that complete the word in each sentence.
3 ✏ Print the letters on the line.

1. The breeze will bl __OW__ the leaves.

| ou (ow) oy |

2. I live in that white h _____ se.

| oy oi ou |

3. Look at the man in the m _____ n!

| oy oo ou |

4. Dad will take the c _____ to the barn.

| oi oy ow |

5. We ate beef st _____ for lunch.

| oi ew ow |

6. He will h _____ l the toys in a sack.

| au ow oi |

7. There is a h _____ k in the nest.

| ew ow aw |

8. We got br _____ d at the store.

| aw ea au |

9. The ball is r _____ nd.

| oi ou oy |

10. Her v _____ ce is very pretty.

| ow oi ou |

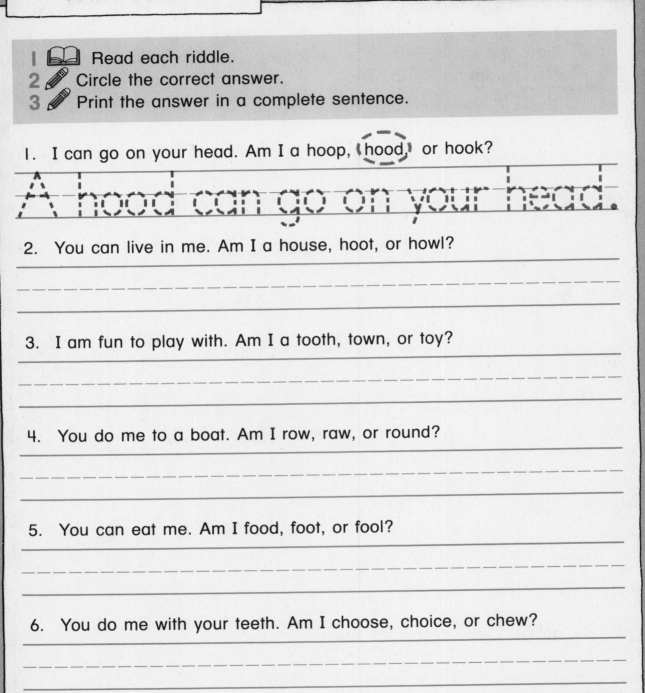

Unit Review: other vowel sounds

1 📖 Read each riddle.
2 ✏️ Circle the correct answer.
3 ✏️ Print the answer in a complete sentence.

1. I can go on your head. Am I a hoop, (hood,) or hook?

A hood can go on your head.

2. You can live in me. Am I a house, hoot, or howl?

_____

3. I am fun to play with. Am I a tooth, town, or toy?

_____

4. You do me to a boat. Am I row, raw, or round?

_____

5. You can eat me. Am I food, foot, or fool?

_____

6. You do me with your teeth. Am I choose, choice, or chew?

_____

7. You can mend a shirt with me. Am I a thread, threw, or throw?

_____

Unit review: using riddles to identify words and write sentences with vowel digraphs and diphthongs

1 📖 Read the words in the box. 2 📖 Read each clue.
3 ✏️ Print the correct word in the puzzle.

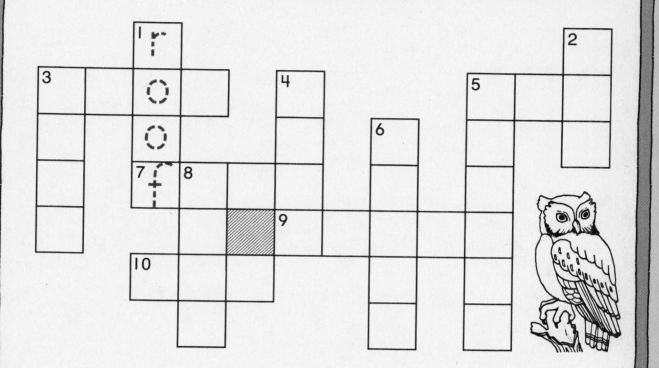

cook   look   roof   tow   owl   thread
coin   boy   paws   sauce   house   flew

ACROSS

3. This is a way to fix food.
5. This is a way to pull a car.
7. If you went in a plane, you ____.
9. You can put this on food.
10. This is not a girl.

DOWN

1. This is on top of a house.
2. This is a wise bird.
3. A dime is one of these.
4. A cat walks on these.
5. You can use this to mend a skirt.
6. This is a place to live.
8. You do this to see.

1 📖 Read the story below.　2 🖐 Say each word.
3 👂 Listen carefully to the vowel sounds.
4 ✏️ Draw a line under words with the sounds of
au, aw, ea, ew, oi, oo, ou, ow, and **oy** you have learned.

One day, I went to a <u>clown</u> <u>show</u>.
I saw a little boy clown bow to the crowd.
He bowed so low, his hat flew off.

I saw a grown-up clown scoot around on a toy auto.
When he came to a pool of oil, he sat down!
Then he ate bread from a bowl with a spoon.

The clowns put balloons on their heads.
One balloon flew up to the roof.
Then it popped with a loud noise.

I enjoyed the clown show.
Maybe I will be a clown when I grow up.

1 📖 Read each question about the story.
2 ✏️ Fill in the space by the correct answer.

1. The little boy clown
   ○ rode a toy auto.
   ● bowed to the crowd.
   ○ ate bread with a spoon.
   ○ blew up balloons.

2. Who or what sat in a pool?
   ○ the little boy clown
   ○ the toy auto
   ○ the grown-up clown
   ○ the balloons

3. Who or what made a loud noise?
   ○ the toy auto
   ○ the crowd
   ○ the bowl and spoon
   ○ the balloon

4. Which is the best title for this story?
   ○ "The Clown Show"
   ○ "A Scoot on an Auto"
   ○ "A Pool of Oil"
   ○ "Balloons on the Roof"

Unit review: reading a story with words with vowel digraphs and diphthongs; story comprehension

au aw ea ew oi oo ou ow oy

Directions: Fill in the space next to the letters that will complete the word.

Example

- ○ ou
- ○ ea
- ○ oy

j___

1.
- ○ ea
- ○ ow
- ○ oi

c___

2.
- ○ oi
- ○ ew
- ○ oo

___l

3.
- ○ aw
- ○ oy
- ○ oo

n___n

4.
- ○ au
- ○ oy
- ○ ou

t___

5.
- ○ ou
- ○ oi
- ○ aw

l___d

6.
- ○ oy
- ○ ow
- ○ ou

sn___

7.
- ○ oi
- ○ ou
- ○ aw

r___

8.
- ○ au
- ○ ew
- ○ oy

h___l

9.
- ○ ea
- ○ aw
- ○ ou

r___d

10.
- ○ ou
- ○ oy
- ○ ow

gr___

11.
- ○ ow
- ○ ea
- ○ oi

h___d

12.
- ○ oy
- ○ ou
- ○ ow

sl___

13.
- ○ ou
- ○ oi
- ○ aw

n___se

14.
- ○ oo
- ○ ow
- ○ oi

h___k

15.
- ○ ou
- ○ oy
- ○ aw

p___

16.
- ○ aw
- ○ oy
- ○ ea

b___

17.
- ○ oo
- ○ ou
- ○ oy

m___n

18.
- ○ oy
- ○ ou
- ○ ew

bl___

19.
- ○ ou
- ○ oo
- ○ oi

c___k

20.
- ○ oi
- ○ ou
- ○ au

m___se

Testing vowel digraphs and diphthongs; using an adapted standardized test format

Compound Words

A compound word is a word made up of two smaller words.

bath + tub = bathtub

1 📖 Read the words for the picture names.
2 ✏️ Print the words together to make a compound word.

foot + ball = football

bird + house = _____

note + book = _____

meat + loaf = _____

mail + box = _____

tree + top = _____

rain + coat = _____

Introducing compound words

Compound Words

1 🗣 Say each picture name.
2 👂 Listen to the sound of each word in the compound word.
3 ✏ Find the spelling of the compound word in the box below and print it under its picture.

popcorn	firewood	bathtub	peanut	rowboat	beehive
shoelace	goldfish	baseball	oatmeal	doghouse	snowfall

popcorn

Compound Words

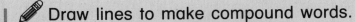

1. ✏️ Draw lines to make compound words.
2. 📖 Read each sentence below.
3. ✏️ Print the compound word that completes the sentence.

air	way
out	plane
drive	boat
row	side

butter	time
bed	bag
hand	end
week	fly

1. The 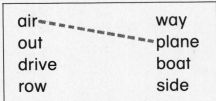 airplane _____ will land on time.

2. I will play _____ in the yard.

3. Mandy left her _____ in the car.

4. We will fish from the _____.

5. I will catch a _____ in my net.

6. Dad reads a story to me at _____.

7. Mom put the car in the _____.

8. Larry will go to a show this _____.

166   Using language arts; forming compound words; using sentence context to select compound words

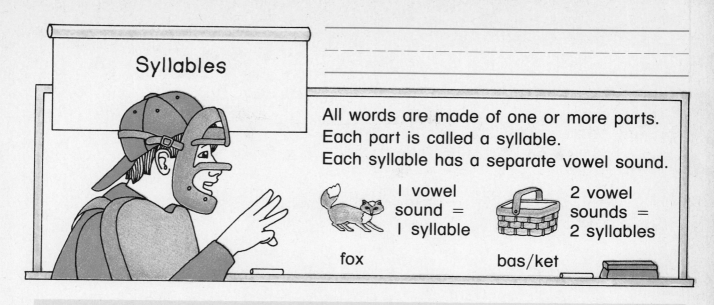

Syllables

All words are made of one or more parts.
Each part is called a syllable.
Each syllable has a separate vowel sound.

1 vowel sound = 1 syllable

fox

2 vowel sounds = 2 syllables

bas/ket

1. Say each picture name.
2. Listen to the syllables.
3. Print the number of syllables you hear.

bed	baby	window	rake
rocket	kite	box	dragon
fan	puppy	seven	cheese
lemon	pillow	pilot	cube
rabbit	cup	soap	robot

Introducing syllables

Syllables

When **le** follows a consonant, the three letters make a syllable.

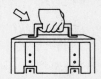 han/dle

1. 👄 Say each picture name. 2. 👂 Listen to the syllables.
3. ✏️ Print the number of syllables you hear.

apple 2	turtle ___	candle ___	file ___
steeple ___	thimble ___	eagle ___	sale ___
tile ___	circle ___	ankle ___	huddle ___
bugle ___	beetle ___	puzzle ___	whale ___
tumble ___	mole ___	puddle ___	juggle ___

168

Syllables

When a vowel comes at the end of a syllable, the vowel sound is usually long.

maple = mā/ple

1 📖 Look at each word and mark the first vowel if it is long.
2 🗣 Say the word.   3 ✏️ Draw a line from each word to its picture.

pī/lot

can/dle

ba/by

pud/dle

thim/ble

bu/gle

win/dow

ti/ger

puz/zle

ro/bot

rab/bit

ze/bra

tum/ble

lem/on

pa/per

ap/ple

1 📖 Read the words in the box.
2 👂 Listen to the two syllables in each word.
3 📖 Read each sentence below.
4 ✏️ Print the word from the box that makes sense in each sentence.

apple	zebra	puddle	rabbit
bugle	lemon	paper	juggle

1. Marta likes to play the 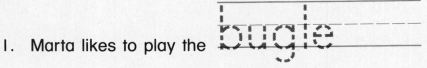 bugle

2. Do you need _____ to write on?

3. Carla will squeeze some _____ on her fish.

4. We have an _____ tree in our backyard.

5. The _____ has white and black stripes.

6. Jacob likes to pet his baby _____

7. The bulldog sat in a _____ of water.

8. Can you _____ three balls at a time?

Reviewing Compound Words and Syllables

1 Say the name of each picture.
2 Listen to the syllables in the name.
3 Find the word for the name of each picture.
4 Draw a line from the picture to its word.

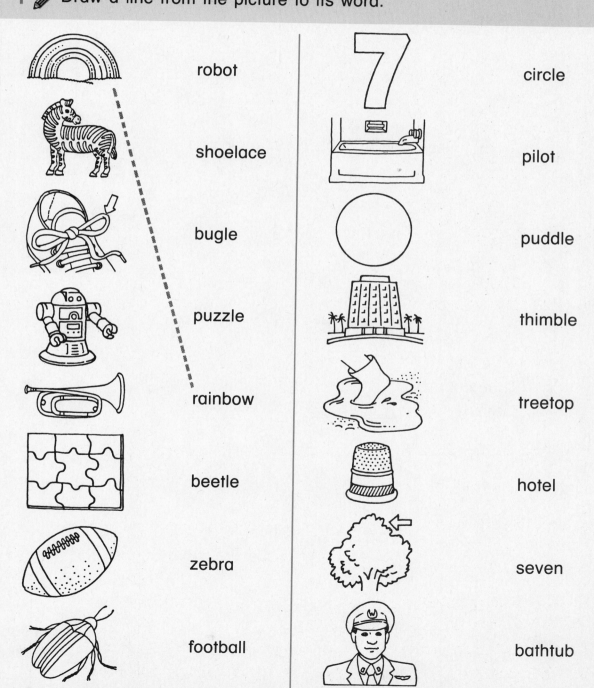

robot

shoelace

bugle

puzzle

rainbow

beetle

zebra

football

circle

pilot

puddle

thimble

treetop

hotel

seven

bathtub

Compound Words and Syllables

Directions: Say each picture name.
Listen to the sound of the syllables in
the name. Fill in the space by the word
for the picture name.

Example

- ○ lemon
- ○ letter
- ○ ladder

1. ○ rattle ○ rabbit ○ robot	2. ○ battle ○ baseball ○ football	3. ○ pilot ○ pile ○ puddle
4. ○ summer ○ sometime ○ sunshine	5. ○ paddle ○ paper ○ painter	6. ○ bugle ○ beetle ○ beets
7. ○ goldfish ○ goldbug ○ goodby	8. ○ sailor ○ sailboat ○ silly	9. ○ tumble ○ table ○ thimble
10. ○ bottle ○ batter ○ boxtop	11. ○ puddle ○ puzzle ○ pepper	12. ○ rattle ○ robot ○ rosebud
13. ○ rainbow ○ bowtie ○ rainfall	14. ○ drop ○ drag ○ dragon	15. ○ birdbath ○ beetle ○ beehive

Testing compound words and syllables; using an adapted standardized test format

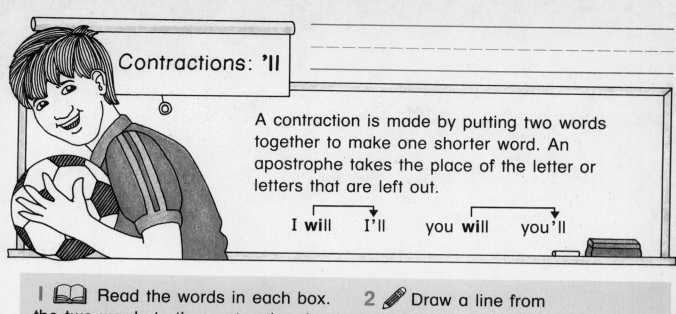

Contractions: 'll

A contraction is made by putting two words together to make one shorter word. An apostrophe takes the place of the letter or letters that are left out.

I **wi**ll → I'll   you **wi**ll → you'll

---

1 📖 Read the words in each box.   2 ✏️ Draw a line from the two words to the contraction that means the same.

I will — — —	he'll	she will	they'll
you will	I'll	it will	she'll
he will	you'll	we will	it'll
		they will	we'll

---

1 📖 Read the words below.   2 ✏️ Print the contraction for the words.

it will

it'll

I will

_____

you will

_____

we will

_____

they will

_____

she will

_____

---

1 📖 Read each contraction below.
2 ✏️ Print the words for each contraction.

he'll

he will

we'll

_____

I'll

_____

you'll

_____

it'll

_____

they'll

_____

Contractions: 'll

1 📖 Read each sentence.
2 ✏️ Print the contraction that completes the sentence.

1. It looks like __it'll__ rain.

| we'll it'll |

2. Ann says _____ take the bus.

| it'll she'll |

3. _____ both be at the party.

| They'll I'll |

4. Grandma hopes _____ all visit soon.

| he'll we'll |

5. I'll run in the race if _____ run, too.

| we'll you'll |

6. Ed says _____ play after school.

| it'll he'll |

7. If you bring a bat, _____ bring a ball.

| I'll it'll |

8. I think _____ be fun to go to camp.

| she'll it'll |

9. Dad says _____ buy us a dog.

| we'll he'll |

10. _____ set up the circus at the school.

| They'll It'll |

Contractions: n't

A contraction is made by putting two words together to make one shorter word. An apostrophe takes the place of the letter or letters that are left out.

did n**o**t   didn't   were n**o**t   weren't

One contraction you need to remember is **won't**. It stands for **will not**.

1 📖 Read the words in each box.   2 ✏️ Draw a line from the two words to the contraction that means the same.

have not	hadn't	is not	wasn't	do not	didn't
has not	haven't	are not	aren't	did not	doesn't
had not	hasn't	was not	isn't	does not	don't

were not	weren't	could not	wouldn't
will not	can't	would not	couldn't
can not	won't	should not	shouldn't

1 📖 Read the words below.   2 ✏️ Print the contraction for the words.

have not	are not	is not
haven't		

was not	were not	did not

do not	could not	does not

has not	had not	will not

Contractions: **n't**

1 📖 Read each sentence.
2 ✏️ Print the contraction that completes the sentence.

1. Jim _isn't_ in his room now.

  isn't hasn't

2. I _____ know where you live.

  wasn't don't

3. Liz and Amy _____ find their books.

  aren't couldn't

4. Sue _____ come over to play.

  can't haven't

5. She _____ let me ride her bike.

  weren't won't

6. Dean _____ been on a jet.

  hasn't don't

7. They _____ going to swim today.

  aren't didn't

8. Tom _____ ready on time.

  can't wasn't

9. You know you _____ tell a lie.

  shouldn't weren't

10. Joy _____ live on this street.

  isn't doesn't

A contraction is made by putting two words together to make one shorter word. An apostrophe takes the place of the letter or letters that are left out.

I **a**m → I'm   he **is** → he's   we **a**re → we're

1 📖 Read the words in each box.   **2** ✏️ Draw a line from the two words to the contraction that means the same.

I am	you're	he is	that's
you are	I'm	she is	she's
we are	they're	it is	it's
they are	we're	that is	he's

1 📖 Read the words below.   **2** ✏️ Print the contraction for the words.

she **is**

she's

that **is**

they **a**re

I **a**m

you **a**re

it **is**

he **is**

we **a**re

1 📖 Read each contraction below.
2 ✏️ Print the words for each contraction.

you're

you are

I'm

it's

she's

we're

that's

1 📖 Read each sentence.
2 ✏️ Print the contraction that completes the sentence.

1. I hope <u>you're</u> in my class.

| that's you're |

2. Mimi will come when _____ ready.

| she's it's |

3. I don't know if _____ going to snow.

| he's it's |

4. _____ singing in the spring show.

| That's I'm |

5. I think _____ a silly hat.

| he's that's |

6. _____ all going to the fair.

| We're She's |

7. Ken and Tina said _____ leaving.

| that's they're |

8. Ben is glad _____ in third grade.

| he's it's |

9. _____ very hot in here.

| It's That's |

10. Do you like this bike _____ riding?

| that's I'm |

Using language arts; using sentence context to select contractions with **'m**, **'s**, **'re**

Contractions: 've, 's

A contraction is made by putting two words together to make one shorter word. An apostrophe takes the place of the letter or letters that are left out.

I **ha**ve → I've   she **ha**s → she's   let **us** → let's

---

1 📖 Read the words in each box.   2 ✏️ Draw a line from the two words to the contraction that means the same.

I have	you've	she has	it's
you have	we've	he has	let's
we have	I've	it has	she's
they have	they've	let us	he's

---

1 📖 Read the words below.   2 ✏️ Print the contraction for the words.

I have

I've

let us

we have

you have

they have

he has

it has

she has

---

1 📖 Read each contraction below.
2 ✏️ Print the words for each contraction.

they've

they have

I've

let's

we've

it's

he's

Introducing contractions with 've, 's

1 📖 Read each sentence.
2 ✏️ Print the contraction that completes the sentence.

1. **Let's** _____ go to the store.

| I've Let's |

2. I know _____ seen you before.

| you've I've |

3. _____ never seen snow!

| They've Let's |

4. _____ been to the zoo.

| We've Let's |

5. _____ made a fort.

| She's It's |

6. Dad says _____ got to come home.

| let's I've |

7. I think _____ found the lost cat.

| they've let's |

8. _____ just had lunch.

| Let's He's |

9. I see _____ saved me a seat.

| you've I've |

10. _____ play hide and seek.

| They've Let's |

Using language arts; using sentence context to select contractions with 've, 's

Reviewing Contractions

1 📖 Read the story below.   2 🗣 Say each word.
3 👂 Listen carefully for the contractions.
4 ✏️ Draw a line under each contraction.

"Don't you just love days like this?" asked Mom.

"No," said Willy, "I've always hated rainy days.
I can't play outside when it rains."

"Willy, it's silly for you to be mad," said Mom.
"If it didn't rain, our roses would die.
You'll feel better if you think about that."

Willy looked at his mom.
"I'm happy for the roses," he said.
"I've been happy for them for days.
But they need sun, too.
So now I think it's time for some sun.
Then I'll be happy for the roses and for me."

1 📖 Read each question about the story.
2 ✏️ Fill in the space by the correct answer.

1. Why does Willy hate rainy days?
   ○ He can play outside.
   ○ He likes the roses.
   ● He can't play outside.
   ○ He hates the roses.

2. What does Mom tell Willy?
   ○ to be happy for her
   ○ to think about himself
   ○ that roses need rain
   ○ to think about the sun

3. What does Willy tell his mom?
   ○ that it's time for some rain
   ○ that roses need sun, too
   ○ that he doesn't like roses
   ○ that roses don't need rain

4. Which is the best title for this story?
   ○ "A Rainy Day"
   ○ "The Happy Roses"
   ○ "Willy Needs the Rain"
   ○ "Mom Loves Roses"

Contractions

Directions: Fill in the space next to
the contraction that means the same
as the words.

Example

- ○ cou'dnt
- ○ couldn't
- ○ coul'not

could not

---

1. ○ Iw'l
   ○ I'l
   ○ I'll

   I will

2. ○ hav't
   ○ haven't
   ○ hav'nt

   have not

3. ○ I'm
   ○ I'am
   ○ Im

   I am

4. ○ ca'nt
   ○ can't
   ○ can'ot

   cannot

---

5. ○ we'l
   ○ we'il
   ○ we'll

   we will

6. ○ don't
   ○ do'nt
   ○ do't

   do not

7. ○ youa'r
   ○ you're
   ○ your'e

   you are

8. ○ hasn't
   ○ has'nt
   ○ has'ot

   has not

---

9. ○ is'nt
   ○ isn't
   ○ is't

   is not

10. ○ I've
    ○ Ih've
    ○ Iv'e

    I have

11. ○ youw'l
    ○ you'll
    ○ you'il

    you will

12. ○ did'nt
    ○ did't
    ○ didn't

    did not

---

13. ○ sh's
    ○ she's
    ○ sh'es

    she is

14. ○ theyw'l
    ○ the'll
    ○ they'll

    they will

15. ○ its
    ○ it's
    ○ it'is

    it is

16. ○ we're
    ○ wer'e
    ○ we'r

    we are

---

17. ○ was'nt
    ○ wasn't
    ○ was't

    was not

18. ○ hw'll
    ○ he'l
    ○ he'll

    he will

19. ○ we'hve
    ○ we've
    ○ we'v

    we have

20. ○ tha'ts
    ○ that's
    ○ tha's

    that is

Testing contractions; using an adapted standardized test format

Plurals: **s**, **es**

A plural is a word that means more than one.

To make a word plural, you usually add **s**. If a word ends in **ch**, **sh**, **s**, or **x**, add **es** to make the word plural.

cat   cat**s**   lunch   lunch**es**

1 📖 Read each base word.   2 ✏️ Add the correct ending to make the base word plural. Print the plural word.

1. hen   hens

2. bus

3. glass

4. box

5. match

6. horse

7. bush

8. bike

9. porch

10. fox

11. path

12. dress

13. duck

14. tax

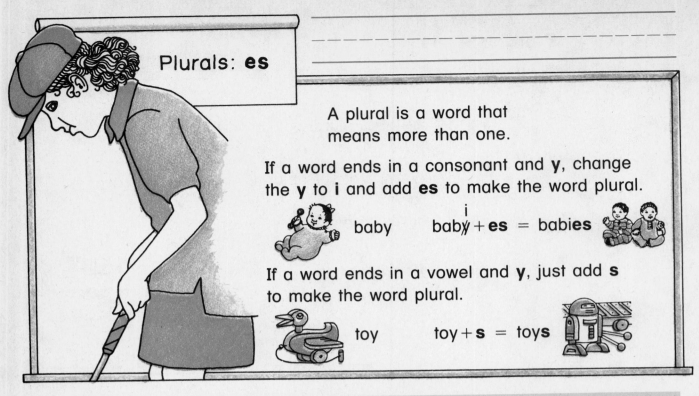

Plurals: es

A plural is a word that means more than one.

If a word ends in a consonant and **y**, change the **y** to **i** and add **es** to make the word plural.

baby   bab$\cancel{y}$ + **es** = babi**es**

If a word ends in a vowel and **y**, just add **s** to make the word plural.

toy   toy + **s** = toy**s**

---

1 📖 Read each base word.   2 ✏️ Add the correct ending to make the base word plural. Print the plural word.

1. pony   ponies

2. penny

3. daisy

4. party

5. toy

6. sky

7. key

8. berry

9. tray

10. county

11. fairy

12. monkey

13. body

14. boy

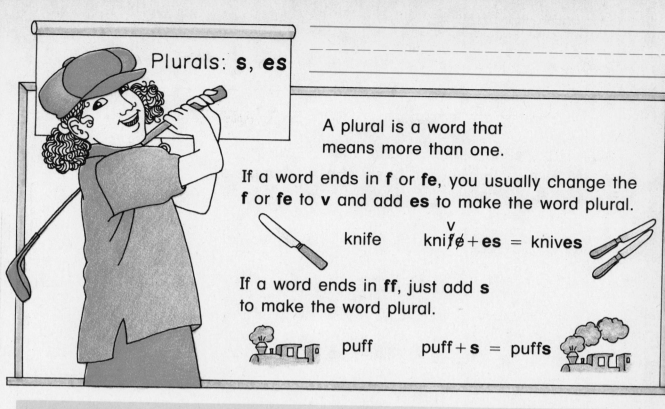

Plurals: **s, es**

A plural is a word that means more than one.

If a word ends in **f** or **fe**, you usually change the **f** or **fe** to **v** and add **es** to make the word plural.

knife   kni~~fe~~ + **es** = kniv**es**

If a word ends in **ff**, just add **s** to make the word plural.

puff   puff + **s** = puff**s**

1 📖 Read each base word.   2 ✏️ Add the correct ending to make the base word plural. Print the plural word.

1. half   halves

2. life

3. puff

4. leaf

5. calf

6. loaf

7. cuff

8. scarf

9. shelf

10. elf

11. cliff

12. wife

13. thief

14. hoof

Reviewing Plurals

1 📖 Read each sentence and base word.
2 ✏️ Write the plural of the base word to complete the sentence.

1. How many **counties** are in this state?

2. The _____ lined up their teams.

3. Martha found these _____ in the hall.

4. Ted won three _____ to the boat show.

5. Don has four hundred _____ in his bank.

6. We saw the cubs playing in the _____ .

7. We saw the _____ swing from the trees.

8. The birds were diving from the _____ .

9. Many babies like to play with _____ .

10. Sally read two _____ before bedtime.

| county |
| coach |
| scarf |
| pass |
| penny |
| bush |
| monkey |
| cliff |
| block |
| story |

Plurals

Directions: Read the base word. Fill in the space next to the plural for that word.

Example

- ○ shelfs
- ○ shelves
- ○ shelfves

shelf

1. ○ homs ○ hommes ○ homes home	2. ○ pennys ○ pennies ○ pennyies penny	3. ○ wishes ○ wishs ○ wishies wish	4. ○ buses ○ busses ○ buss bus
5. ○ partys ○ parties ○ partyes party	6. ○ birdies ○ birdes ○ birds bird	7. ○ wolfs ○ wolves ○ wolfies wolf	8. ○ blockes ○ blockies ○ blocks block
9. ○ boxes ○ boxs ○ boxies box	10. ○ cufs ○ cuffs ○ cufves cuff	11. ○ hands ○ handes ○ handies hand	12. ○ monkies ○ monkeys ○ monkees monkey
13. ○ wives ○ wiffes ○ wifes wife	14. ○ foxies ○ foxs ○ foxes fox	15. ○ puppes ○ puppyies ○ puppies puppy	16. ○ girls ○ girles ○ girlies girl
17. ○ lunches ○ lunchies ○ lunchs lunch	18. ○ halfs ○ halves ○ halvies half	19. ○ cliffs ○ clifves ○ cliffes cliff	20. ○ glasss ○ glassies ○ glasses glass

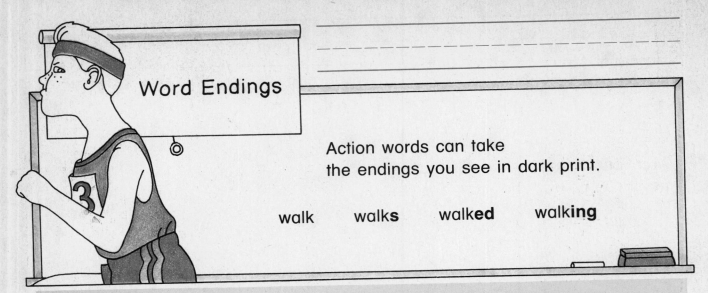

Word Endings

Action words can take
the endings you see in dark print.

walk   walk**s**   walk**ed**   walk**ing**

I 📖 Read each base word.   2 ✏️ Add the ending in dark print
to the base word. Print the new word on the line.

	s or es	ed	ing
1. play	plays	played	playing
2. pull			
3. wash			
4. jump			
5. talk			
6. pass			
7. wait			
8. reach			
9. sound			

Introducing inflected endings: **s, es, ed, ing**

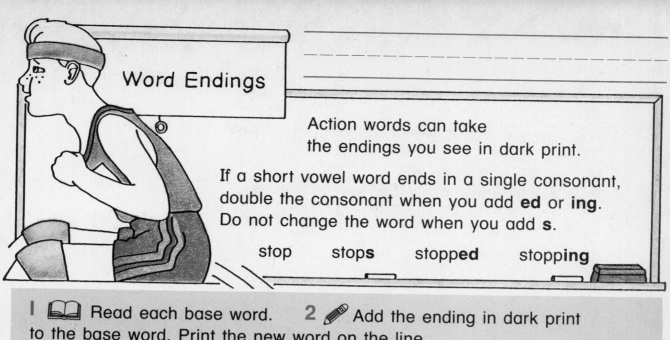

Word Endings

Action words can take
the endings you see in dark print.

If a short vowel word ends in a single consonant,
double the consonant when you add **ed** or **ing**.
Do not change the word when you add **s**.

stop   stop**s**   stopp**ed**   stopp**ing**

1 📖 Read each base word.   **2** ✏️ Add the ending in dark print
to the base word. Print the new word on the line.

	s	**ed**	**ing**
1. clap	claps	clapped	clapping
2. trim			
3. tug			
4. mop			
5. beg			
6. rip			
7. pet			
8. hug			
9. hop			

Introducing inflected endings: **s**, **ed**, **ing**; doubling the final consonant

Word Endings

1 📖 Read each sentence.
2 ✏️ Print the word that makes sense in the sentence.

1. Steve _walks_ to school.

| walking walks |

2. The tire _____ down the hill.

| rolled rolling |

3. The team is _____ to go to the park.

| begged begging |

4. Kim _____ birds for hours each day.

| watching watches |

5. Pam _____ the math prize every year.

| winning wins |

6. Carl _____ by this way last week.

| passed passing |

7. The girls _____ for their coats.

| reached reaches |

8. The child is _____ the puppy.

| petted petting |

9. The dogs _____ their tails at us.

| wagged wags |

10. Are you _____ a tune?

| hummed humming |

190

Using language arts; using sentence context to select words with inflected endings: **s**, **es**, **ed**, **ing**

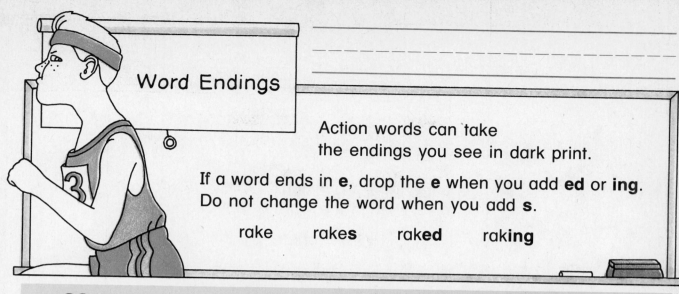

Word Endings

Action words can take
the endings you see in dark print.

If a word ends in **e**, drop the **e** when you add **ed** or **ing**.
Do not change the word when you add **s**.

rake   rake**s**   rak**ed**   rak**ing**

1 📖 Read each base word.   2 ✏️ Add the ending in dark print to the base word. Print the new word on the line.

	s	ed	ing
1. hope	hopes	hoped	hoping
2. move			
3. smile			
4. rule			
5. use			
6. hike			
7. rope			
8. skate			
9. dance			

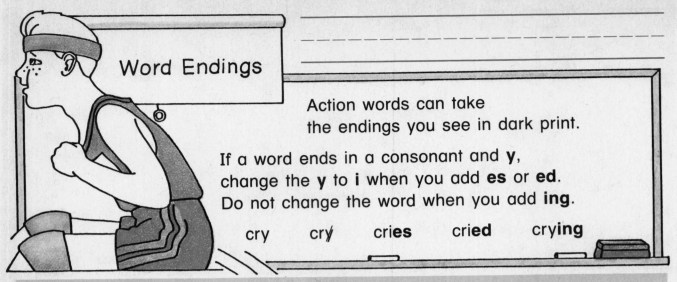

Word Endings

Action words can take
the endings you see in dark print.

If a word ends in a consonant and **y**,
change the **y** to **i** when you add **es** or **ed**.
Do not change the word when you add **ing**.

cry cry cri**es** cri**ed** cry**ing**

1 📖 Read each base word. 2 ✏️ Add the ending in dark print
to the base word. Print the new word on the line.

es	ed	ing
tries	**tried**	**trying**

1. try

2. dry

3. study

4. cry

5. copy

6. hurry

7. fry

8. carry

9. worry

192

Word Endings

1 📖 Read each sentence.
2 ✏️ Print the word that makes sense in the sentence.

1. Rosa **hopes** she will get a new bike.

| hoped   hopes |

2. I always _____ my book in a backpack.

| carrying   carried |

3. Mom is _____ chicken for dinner.

| fried   frying |

4. Susan _____ her bike to school.

| riding   rides |

5. The baby _____ at me.

| smiled   smiling |

6. We _____ on the sidewalk.

| skated   skates |

7. I saw Lee _____ to the bus.

| hurries   hurrying |

8. The baby _____ when she is hungry.

| crying   cries |

9. Mel _____ up the food he dropped.

| mopped   mopping |

10. Carlos _____ every day.

| studying   studies |

1 📖 Read each base word.
2 ✏️ Add the ending in dark print to the base word and
print the new word on the line.

s or es	ed	ing
1. hop	hops	hopped	hopping
2. wash			
3. love			
4. watch			
5. cry			
6. shout			
7. hurry			
8. trot			
9. pass			

Reviewing inflected endings

Word Endings

Directions: Read the base word. Fill in the space next to the word with the correct spelling of the base word and ending.

Example

- ○ studing
- ○ studying
- ○ studdying

study

1. ○ clapping ○ claping ○ clappying clap	2. ○ studied ○ studyied ○ studded study	3. ○ moveing ○ moving ○ movving move	4. ○ helpied ○ helpped ○ helped help
5. ○ marryed ○ married ○ marryied marry	6. ○ plays ○ plais ○ playes play	7. ○ hoping ○ hopping ○ hopeing hope	8. ○ moppied ○ moped ○ mopped mop
9. ○ ripped ○ riped ○ ripied rip	10. ○ hurrys ○ hurries ○ huries hurry	11. ○ jumpped ○ jumpied ○ jumped jump	12. ○ rubbing ○ rubing ○ rubbying rub
13. ○ smilled ○ smiled ○ smilied smile	14. ○ hugging ○ huging ○ huggin hug	15. ○ trys ○ tryes ○ tries try	16. ○ riding ○ ridding ○ rideing ride
17. ○ wining ○ winning ○ winying win	18. ○ skatted ○ skatied ○ skated skate	19. ○ useing ○ using ○ ussing use	20. ○ reaching ○ reachhing ○ reachying reach

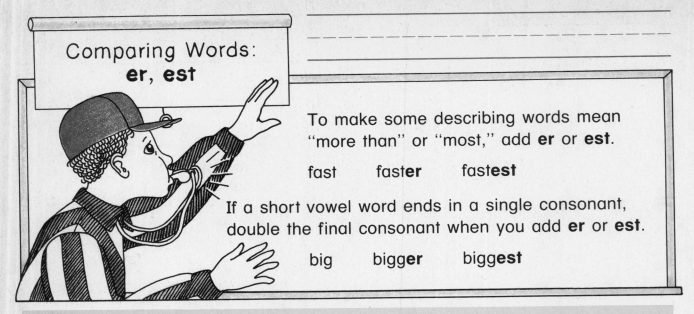

Comparing Words: er, est

To make some describing words mean "more than" or "most," add **er** or **est**.

fast   fast**er**   fast**est**

If a short vowel word ends in a single consonant, double the final consonant when you add **er** or **est**.

big   bigg**er**   bigg**est**

1 📖 Read each base word.   **2** ✏️ Add the ending in dark print to the base word. Print the new word on the line.

	er	est
1. dim	*dimmer*	*dimmest*
2. mad		
3. smart		
4. fat		
5. long		
6. hot		
7. flat		
8. fast		

Introducing comparatives: **er**, **est**; doubling the final consonant

Comparing Words: er, est

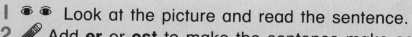

1 👁👁 Look at the picture and read the sentence.
2 ✏️ Add **er** or **est** to make the sentence make sense.
Double the final consonant as needed.

1. The cat is fat ‾ter‾ than the dog.

2. Chuck is the short _____ .

3. Sally is fast _____ than Mark.

4. I think Mandy is the old _____ .

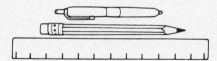

5. The ruler is the long _____ .

6. The knife is flat _____ than the spoon.

7. My bunny is the soft _____ .

8. A monkey is smart _____ than a camel.

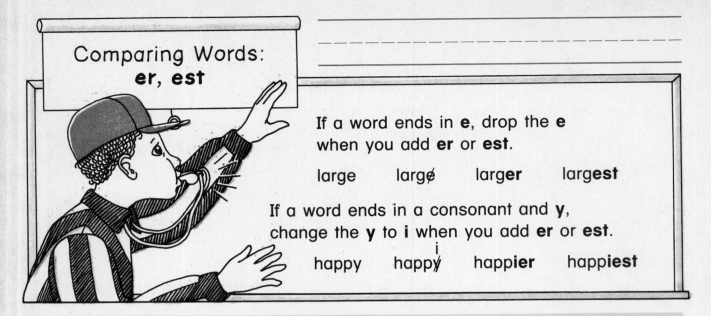

Comparing Words: er, est

If a word ends in **e**, drop the **e** when you add **er** or **est**.

large   larg~~e~~   larg**er**   larg**est**

If a word ends in a consonant and **y**, change the **y** to **i** when you add **er** or **est**.

happy   happ~~y~~   happ**ier**   happ**iest**

1 📖 Read each base word.   2 ✏️ Add the ending in dark print to the base word. Print the new word on the line.

	er	est
1. white	whiter	whitest
2. busy		
3. jolly		
4. ripe		
5. late		
6. sorry		
7. nice		
8. furry		

Introducing comparatives: **er**, **est**; dropping the final **e**, changing **y** to **i**

Comparing Words:
er, est

1 📖 Look at the picture and read the sentence.
2 ✏️ Add **er** or **est** to the base word to make the sentence
make sense. Drop the final **e** or change **y** to **i** as needed.

Your teacher is the wisest person at the party.

| wise |

One dress is much _____ than the other one.

| fine |

Mr. March is the _____ man I know.

| jolly |

This paint is _____ than that one.

| white |

That shark is the _____ one of all.

| scary |

Your rabbit is the _____ of the three.

| large |

We are _____ now than we were this morning.

| busy |

Marta is _____ than her pal Sally.

| happy |

Reviewing Comparing Words

1 📖 Read each sentence.
2 ✏️ Circle the word that makes sense in the sentence.
3 ✏️ Print it on the line.

1. I think a rose is **prettier** than a tulip.

   pretty (prettier) prettiest

2. Herb is _____ than Tom.

   heavy   heavier   heaviest

3. Joy is the _____ girl on our team.

   tall   taller   tallest

4. It is _____ in July than in March.

   hot   hotter   hottest

5. Ned's room is _____ than Dan's room.

   tidy   tidier   tidiest

6. Those sheep have the _____ wool I have seen.

   fine   finer   finest

7. We sat down to rest on the _____ rock we could find.

   flat   flatter   flattest

Comparing Words

Directions: Read the base word. Fill in the space next to the word with the correct spelling of the base word and **er** or **est**.

Example

○ furryier
○ furrier
○ furyier
furry

1. ○ wetter ○ weter ○ wettier wet	2. ○ paleest ○ palest ○ pallest pale	3. ○ busyier ○ busyer ○ busier busy	4. ○ smartest ○ smarttest ○ smartiest smart
5. ○ fastest ○ fasttest ○ fastiest fast	6. ○ rippest ○ ripest ○ ripiest ripe	7. ○ longest ○ longgest ○ longiest long	8. ○ sunnyier ○ sunier ○ sunnier sunny
9. ○ shortter ○ shorter ○ shortier short	10. ○ curlyier ○ curllier ○ curlier curly	11. ○ safest ○ saffest ○ safeest safe	12. ○ hoter ○ hotter ○ hottier hot
13. ○ dimest ○ dimmiest ○ dimmest dim	14. ○ sillyier ○ sillier ○ silier silly	15. ○ finner ○ fineer ○ finer fine	16. ○ whitest ○ whittest ○ whiteest white
17. ○ sorryier ○ sorrier ○ sorier sorry	18. ○ latest ○ lattest ○ latiest late	19. ○ tallier ○ taller ○ taler tall	20. ○ flattest ○ flatest ○ flattiest flat

Prefixes: re-

A prefix is a word part that is added to the beginning of a word.

The prefix **re-** means "again."

re- + read = reread
Reread means "read again."

1 📖 Read each meaning.   2 ✏️ Print the word for each meaning.

1. pay again   repay   4. do again

2. write again _____   5. use again

3. draw again _____   6. play again

1 ✏️ Add **re-** to each base word on the right.
2 ✏️ Print the new word on the line to complete the sentence.

1. The men will repaint the house.   re paint

2. Mother started to _____ the stew.   _____heat

3. She began to _____ the glasses.   _____fill

4. Dan wants to _____ the tape.   _____use

5. Mrs. Diaz will _____ the movie.   _____run

Prefixes: **un-**

A prefix is a word part that is added to the beginning of a word.

The prefix **un-** can mean "not" or "to do the opposite."

un- + happy = unhappy
Unhappy means "not happy."

1 📖 Read each meaning.   2 ✏️ Print the word for each meaning.

1. not lucky   unlucky

2. not safe   _____

3. not kind   _____

4. do the opposite of tie   _____

5. do the opposite of lock   _____

6. do the opposite of wrap   _____

1 ✏️ Add **un-** to each base word on the right.
2 ✏️ Print the new word on the line to complete the sentence.

1. Maria will   untie   her shoes.   un tie

2. Is it _____ to cut in line?   _____fair

3. Did you _____ the door?   _____lock

4. It is _____ to leave toys on the steps.   _____safe

Suffixes: -ly

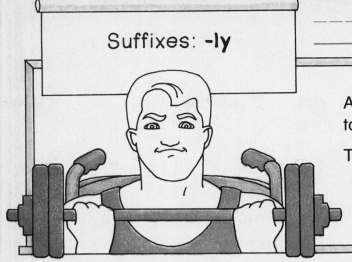

A suffix is a word part that is added to the end of a word.

The suffix **-ly** means "in a way."

slow + **-ly** = slowly
Slowly means "in a slow way."

---

1 📖 Read each meaning.   2 ✏️ Print the word for each meaning.

1. in a quiet way   <u>quietly</u>

2. in a sad way

3. in a nice way

4. in a glad way

5. in a brave way

6. in a neat way

---

1 ✏️ Add **-ly** to each base word on the right.
2 ✏️ Print the new word on the line to complete the sentence.

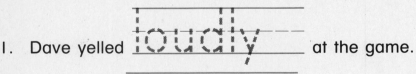

1. Dave yelled <u>loudly</u> at the game.   loud<u>ly</u>

2. Ellen sings _____.   sweet_____

3. The girl spoke _____.   soft_____

4. Joy ran _____ to the store.   quick_____

5. Kip writes _____.   neat_____

Suffixes: -ful

A suffix is a word part that is added to the end of a word.

The suffix **-ful** means "full of."

hope + **-ful** = hopeful
Hopeful means "full of hope."

---

1 📖 Read each meaning.   2 ✏️ Print the word for each meaning.

1. full of cheer   cheerful   4. full of care _____

2. full of play _____   5. full of joy _____

3. full of pain _____   6. full of help _____

---

1 ✏️ Add **-ful** to each base word on the right.
2 ✏️ Print the new word on the line to complete the sentence.

1. It was painful when she hit her toe.   pain **ful**

2. Be _____ when you cross the street.   care____

3. This book is _____.   help____

4. The kitten was _____.   play____

5. It was a _____ place to sit.   cheer____

Reviewing Prefixes and Suffixes

1 📖 Read each sentence.
2 ✏️ Print a word from the box on the line to complete each sentence.

unsafe	playful	retell	cheerful
gladly	reuse	bravely	untie

1. I will _gladly_ help you with your work.

2. It is _____ to play with a tiger.

3. Please _____ that funny story.

4. Help me _____ the rope from the boat.

5. Our little cat stood up _____ to that big dog.

6. Can we _____ this glass jar?

7. That _____ puppy jumped on Carlos.

8. We were glad to see Mom look so _____

Reviewing prefixes and suffixes; using sentence context to select words with **re-**, **un-**, **-ful**, **-ly**

re- un- -ful -ly

Directions: Fill in the space next to the word with only the base word underlined.

Example

- ○ <u>re</u>read
- ○ re<u>read</u>
- ○ <u>reread</u>

1. ○ <u>quickly</u> ○ quick<u>ly</u> ○ <u>quick</u>ly	2. ○ <u>re</u>fill ○ re<u>fill</u> ○ re<u>fill</u>	3. ○ <u>un</u>happy ○ un<u>happy</u> ○ <u>unhappy</u>
4. ○ <u>un</u>wrap ○ un<u>wrap</u> ○ <u>unwrap</u>	5. ○ <u>ne</u>arly ○ near<u>ly</u> ○ <u>near</u>ly	6. ○ hope<u>ful</u> ○ <u>hope</u>ful ○ <u>hopeful</u>
7. ○ re<u>think</u> ○ re<u>think</u> ○ <u>re</u>think	8. ○ <u>playful</u> ○ play<u>ful</u> ○ <u>play</u>ful	9. ○ <u>un</u>lock ○ un<u>lock</u> ○ un<u>lock</u>
10. ○ <u>bra</u>vely ○ brave<u>ly</u> ○ <u>brave</u>ly	11. ○ <u>un</u>kind ○ <u>unkind</u> ○ un<u>kind</u>	12. ○ helpful ○ help<u>ful</u> ○ <u>help</u>ful
13. ○ <u>re</u>use ○ <u>re</u>use ○ re<u>use</u>	14. ○ <u>cheerful</u> ○ cheer<u>ful</u> ○ <u>cheer</u>ful	15. ○ <u>sweet</u>ly ○ sweet<u>ly</u> ○ <u>sweetly</u>

Showing Ownership: 's

Add **'s** to a word to show that something belongs to one person or thing.

The dog has a short tail.

The dog**'s** tail is short.

1 📖 Look at each picture and read the sentence.
2 ✏️ Add **'s** to the underlined word to show ownership.

The <u>girl</u> has a fuzzy coat.

The **girl's** _____ coat is fuzzy.

<u>Kim</u> has a game that is fun to play.

_____ game is fun to play.

The <u>man</u> has an old truck.

The _____ truck is old.

That <u>child</u> has a new toy.

That _____ toy is new.

<u>Tony</u> has a cute puppy.

_____ puppy is cute.

<u>Mary</u> has a broken foot.

_____ foot is broken.

Showing Ownership:
s'

Add ' after the last **s** in a word to show that something belongs to more than one person or thing.

The campers have a green tent.

The campers' tent is green.

---

1 📖 Look at each picture and read the sentence.
2 ✏️ Add ' to the underlined word to show ownership.

The <u>players</u> have a good team.

The **players'** team is good.

The <u>dogs</u> have a bowl full of food.

The _____ bowl is full of food.

The <u>horses</u> have a big field.

The _____ field is big.

The <u>girls</u> have a clean room.

The _____ room is clean.

The <u>kittens</u> have a soft bed.

The _____ bed is soft.

The <u>birds</u> have a nest in the tree.

The _____ nest is in the tree.

Introducing possessives: **s'**

Reviewing Showing Ownership

1 📖 Look at the picture and read each sentence.
2 ✏️ Print a word from the box to complete each sentence.

| girl's | girls' | boy's | boys' | dog's | dogs' | monkey's | monkeys' |

1. The __girls'__ ball went into the street.

2. The _____ cat sat on her lap.

3. The _____ bone was in its mouth.

4. The _____ leashes were very strong.

5. The _____ bike held both of them.

6. The _____ sled was very big.

7. The _____ hat fell from his head.

8. The _____ food was in the tree.

Showing Ownership

Directions: Fill in the space next to the word that would be used to show ownership for the person, people, thing, or things pictured.

Example

- ○ dogs
- ○ dog's
- ○ dogs'

1. ○ kittens ○ kitten's ○ kittens'	**2.** ○ man's ○ men ○ men's	**3.** ○ cats' ○ cats ○ cat's
4. ○ monkey's ○ monkeys' ○ monkeys	**5.** ○ cooks ○ cooks' ○ cook's	**6.** ○ dog's ○ dogs ○ dogs'
7. ○ pig's ○ pigs ○ pigs'	**8.** ○ boys ○ boy's ○ boys'	**9.** ○ nurse's ○ nurses ○ nurses'
10. ○ girl's ○ girls ○ girls'	**11.** ○ clowns ○ clowns' ○ clown's	**12.** ○ seals' ○ seal's ○ seals
13. ○ farmers ○ farmer's ○ farmers'	**14.** ○ goat's ○ goats' ○ goats	**15.** ○ players' ○ players ○ player's

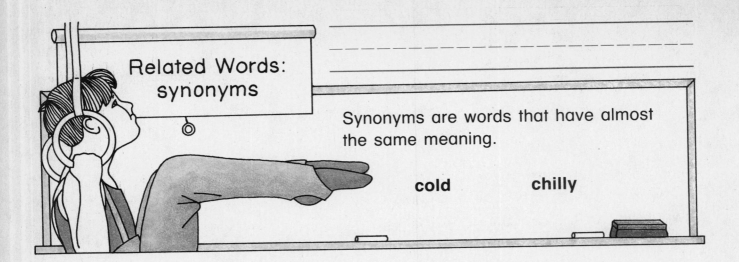

Related Words: synonyms

Synonyms are words that have almost the same meaning.

cold   **chilly**

1 📖 Read the words in each column.
2 ✏️ Draw a line between the words that are synonyms.

unhappy	quick	cheerful	cap
tell	close	chair	shop
fast	little	hat	boat
small	sad	car	seat
go	say	store	happy
shut	leave	ship	auto
rest	house	jet	pal
stone	pick	plant	pot
shout	nap	friend	bush
big	rock	shore	plane
choose	large	noise	beach
home	yell	pan	sound

Related Words: antonyms

Antonyms are words that have almost opposite meanings.

bad - **good**

1 📖 Read the words in each column.
2 ✏ Draw a line between the words that are antonyms.

hot	little	inside	short
wet	after	top	sick
before	cold	open	outside
sad	dry	well	quiet
big	soft	tall	close
hard	happy	loud	bottom
slow	frown	start	weak
under	far	old	tiny
smile	dirty	huge	up
near	fast	strong	new
unhappy	over	sweet	stop
clean	glad	down	sour

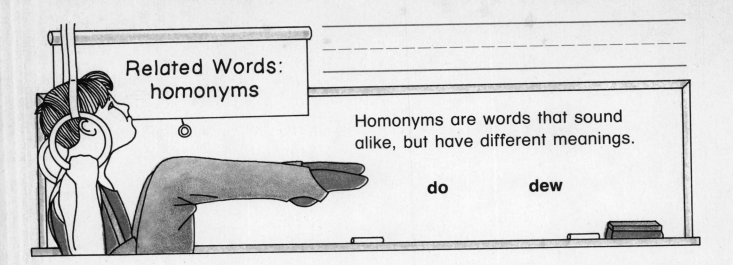

Related Words:
homonyms

Homonyms are words that sound alike, but have different meanings.

do   **dew**

1 📖 Read the words in each column.
2 ✏️ Draw a line between the words that are homonyms.

write	buy	new	would
four	eight	road	know
by	plane	wood	sail
ate	right	our	knew
sent	for	no	hour
plain	cent	sale	rode

meat	tale	pale	stair
I	here	one	to
dear	son	sea	pail
tail	meet	two	won
hear	deer	through	see
sun	eye	stare	threw

Synonyms have almost the same meaning.

cold   chilly

Antonyms have almost opposite meanings.

cold   hot

Homonyms sound alike.

to   too   two

1. 📖 Read both words.
2. ✏️ Print **S** if the words are synonyms. Print **A** if the words are antonyms. Print **H** if the words are homonyms.

1.	huge	large	S	10.	new	old
2.	dear	deer		11.	rock	stone
3.	happy	sad		12.	son	sun
4.	hear	here		13.	by	buy
5.	go	leave		14.	know	no
6.	high	low		15.	short	tall
7.	blue	blew		16.	angry	mad
8.	quick	fast		17.	never	always
9.	to	two		18.	end	stop

1 📖 Read each silly question.
2 ✏️ Print **yes** or **no** to answer the question.

1. Is the beach at the shore?

yes

2. Does **four** mean **for**?

3. Is hot tea cold?

4. Is the new car old?

5. Can a cent be sent?

6. Is a shop a store?

1 📖 Read the words in the box.
2 ✏️ Use words from the box and your own words
to write silly questions of your own.

deer	dear	hear	here	is	does	large	big	tail	tale
knew	new	old	can	rock	stone	a	the	hot	cold
sun	son	good	bad	rode	road	street	on	as	be

1. Can a deer

2.

3.

Unit review: synonyms, antonyms, homonyms; reading and writing sentences with
synonyms, antonyms, homonyms

Synonyms, Antonyms, Homonyms

Directions: Read each pair of words. Fill in the space below the **S** if the words are synonyms. Fill in the space below the **A** if the words are antonyms. Fill in the space below the **H** if the words are homonyms.

Example

		S	A	H
big	small	○	○	○

			S	A	H
1.	blue	blew	○	○	○
2.	loud	quiet	○	○	○
3.	happy	cheerful	○	○	○
4.	tale	tail	○	○	○
5.	near	far	○	○	○
6.	large	big	○	○	○
7.	old	new	○	○	○
8.	fast	quick	○	○	○
9.	hot	cold	○	○	○
10.	tiny	little	○	○	○

			S	A	H
11.	for	four	○	○	○
12.	nap	rest	○	○	○
13.	one	won	○	○	○
14.	sun	son	○	○	○
15.	pal	friend	○	○	○
16.	short	long	○	○	○
17.	hard	soft	○	○	○
18.	to	two	○	○	○
19.	quick	slow	○	○	○
20.	road	rode	○	○	○

Testing synonyms, antonyms, homonyms; using an adapted standardized test format

ABC Order

a b c d e f g h i j k l m n o p q r s t u v w x y z
A B C D E F G H I J K L M N O P Q R S T U V W X Y Z

1. 📖 Read each group of letters.
2. ✏️ Print the letters in ABC order.

b d a c	f h e g	l k i j	q t r s
a b c d			
e c f d	j i h g	r o p q	y w z x
v t u s	o p m n	C F E D	G H F I
S Q R P	K J I H	V X W Y	U W V T
T R S U	K M L J	M O N L	Q P N O

218

ABC Order

1 📖 Read the words in each box.
2 👀 Look at the underlined letter or letters in each word.
3 ✏️ Circle **yes** if the words are in ABC order.
Circle **no** if the words are not in ABC order.

<u>d</u>uck <u>e</u>gg <u>f</u>arm	<u>c</u>oat <u>b</u>aby <u>d</u>ay	<u>h</u>is <u>i</u>s <u>j</u>ust	<u>s</u>top <u>t</u>wo <u>u</u>p
(**yes**)　no	**yes**　no	**yes**　no	**yes**　no
<u>h</u>am <u>h</u>um <u>h</u>im	<u>g</u>ame <u>h</u>ere <u>i</u>n	<u>m</u>ake <u>n</u>ot <u>o</u>ne	<u>s</u>ong <u>s</u>ing <u>s</u>ang
yes　no	**yes**　no	**yes**　no	**yes**　no
<u>o</u>ff <u>n</u>ew <u>p</u>ig	<u>b</u>ird <u>c</u>at <u>d</u>og	<u>t</u>op <u>t</u>ap <u>t</u>ip	<u>r</u>ide <u>s</u>tory <u>t</u>hey
yes　no	**yes**　no	**yes**　no	**yes**　no
<u>e</u>asy <u>f</u>ood <u>g</u>oat	<u>m</u>ore <u>n</u>ext <u>l</u>ost	<u>h</u>air <u>g</u>irl <u>f</u>all	<u>fa</u>n <u>fi</u>n <u>fu</u>n
yes　no	**yes**　no	**yes**　no	**yes**　no

Using dictionary skills; identifying alphabetical sequence in words by first or second letter

ABC Order

Directions: Read the sets of words in each row. Look at the first letter or letters of the words in each set. Fill in the space below the set of words that is in ABC order.

Example

cat ant dog ○	beg bag big ○	map nap over ○	tan sun room ○

I.	egg fan grow ○	stop quick roll ○	hot good frog ○	land man kite ○
2.	crab bone art ○	pay open new ○	sat set sit ○	more lion near ○
3.	shop tire rich ○	dig car bear ○	fat foot fit ○	quick run star ○
4.	many never listen ○	cat coat cut ○	hill fly green ○	bat but bit ○
5.	noon out pig ○	yes zoo win ○	dear blue chair ○	sew saw so ○

Testing dictionary skills: alphabetical sequence; using an adapted standardized test format